Financial Orchestration

Leading Cost, Budget & System Change as a Modern CFO

Dr. Leticia Lilleström

ISBN: 978-91-990472-7-0
Third Edition, 2025
Cover design by Leticia Lillestrom

Where Vision Meets Velocity

In The Strategic CFO (Volume One), we redefined financial leadership for an era shaped by AI, agility, and strategic uncertainty.

In Leadership in the AI Age (Volume Two), we anchored that transformation in what technology cannot replace: judgement, ethics, empathy, and emotional intelligence.

This third volume completes the arc.

Because vision without structure becomes theatre. And even the strongest values struggle to hold under pressure if execution is weak.

Financial Orchestration is the companion volume for CFOs and finance leaders who do not only want to think strategically but build the operating system that makes strategy real.

Inside these pages you will find practical frameworks, adoption-ready templates, and operating rhythms designed to make cost, budgeting, and system change land cleanly across the enterprise.

This book is built for the moments that separate competent finance from leadership-grade finance:

- Redesigning cost centre structures so accountability becomes legible.
- Leading FP&A system transitions without trust breakdown.

- Creating budget ownership that moves beyond compliance into discipline.
- Building dashboards that turn performance signals into timely decisions.
- Designing governance so accountability, escalation, and decision rights remain clear.
- Orchestrating finance under crisis and complexity without losing control of the operating rhythm.

Leadership does not end in the boardroom. It continues in what you build, what you embed, and what you make repeatable, especially when no one is watching.

Let's begin.

How to Use This Book

This volume is designed to be read in two ways. Read it sequentially when you are building or resetting the finance operating system; each chapter moves from strategic intent into operating structure, adoption, governance, and resilience. Use it selectively when you are solving a live problem: the chapter narrative explains the doctrine, while the appendices provide working templates and checklists.

When using a tool, return first to the governing question in the relevant chapter. The templates are not substitutes for judgement. They are structures for making assumptions, ownership, thresholds, and decisions visible enough to challenge.

Where AI or automated models are used, apply the same principle: generated outputs are inputs to a governed decision process. Keep source, ownership, review, and sign-off visible.

Chapter 1: From Strategy to Execution

Where Insight Becomes Infrastructure

There comes a moment in every CFO's journey when vision is no longer the challenge, implementation is.

You've articulated the strategy. You've aligned with the CEO. Your board believes in the financial direction. You've shaped the story, translated it into numbers, anchored it into a plan, and committed it into a forecast.

But nothing changes... until something is built.

Until tools are integrated, timelines are managed, people are trained, and numbers are trusted again. Until departments stop treating finance as a monthly audit and begin experiencing it as a shared operating system. Until leaders see their responsibility reflected back at them not as blame, but as clarity.

Welcome to the space between clarity and completion.

This is where many leaders stall. Not because they lack knowledge, but because operational transformation is a different muscle entirely. It's not glamorous. It isn't rewarded with applause. It doesn't live in the boardroom narrative. It lives in the backstage work that turns intention into repeatable performance, the work that sustains every success behind the curtain.

And here is the uncomfortable truth: strategy fails most often not because it was wrong, but because it was never operationalised. It remained a belief. A document. A slide deck. An announcement. The organisation nodded, updated their language, and returned to the old rhythm.

This book exists because the modern CFO is no longer only asked to design the financial future, they are asked to build the scaffolding that makes that future survivable, measurable, and real.

The Role of the Operational CFO

In Volume One, we made a case for the CFO as a strategic co-pilot, someone who translates insight into foresight. The CFO as a navigator of complexity, a steward of capital, a voice in the room where direction is chosen.

In Volume Two, we elevated the conversation into the human realm, decision-making with empathy, building trust during transformation, recognising that people do not follow spreadsheets; they follow leaders who make uncertainty feel manageable.

Volume Three begins at the edge of those two paths.

Here, the CFO doesn't just guide, they build. Not just the why, but the how. Not just the idea, but the infrastructure that makes it real.

This is not "operational" in the narrow sense of administration. This is operational as architecture, the deliberate design of rhythms, roles, tools, and governance so that strategy becomes behaviour and not theatre.

The Operational CFO leads the mechanics of execution without losing the meaning of the mission. They understand that finance is not merely a scorekeeper; it is the system by which the organisation learns.

In practice, the Operational CFO does five things exceptionally well:

First, they lead cross-functional implementation with structured clarity. Not by dominating decisions, but by building frameworks that make decision-making possible at speed. Clarity is a form of leadership, especially when the organisation is under strain.

Second, they oversee system transitions and cost centre realignments without chaos. They recognise that when finance changes its structures, it is not changing "codes." It is changing how accountability is experienced across the business. A restructure can either increase precision and trust or trigger confusion and resistance that quietly sabotages adoption.

Third, they turn timelines, budgets, and dashboards into tools of organisational orchestration. They stop treating planning artefacts as administrative documents and start treating them as leadership instruments, designed to align behaviour, prioritise attention, and surface truth early.

Fourth, they build confidence in the numbers by building confidence in the process. A forecast is only respected when the organisation trusts how it was produced, updated, and interpreted.

Finally, they hold the most important operational insight: people don't resist change, they resist confusion. They resist unclear expectations, shifting rules, and decisions made in silence. Resistance is frequently a symptom of poor translation, not poor intent.

The Operational CFO becomes, therefore, a translator of intent into structure. And that translation is where executive credibility is either secured or lost.

Executive Case Insight: The Strategy Everyone Agreed With and No One Implemented

It often begins with a perfect moment.

A board meeting ends with alignment. The CEO is energised. The transformation language is strong. A new strategic direction is endorsed: margin restoration, digital acceleration, operational efficiency, a move into new segments, a new commercial model. The CFO presents clean analysis, a credible pathway, a disciplined investment profile, a risk narrative that feels controlled.

And then, quietly, the strategy enters the organisation.

A deck is shared. A leadership memo goes out. A town hall occurs. People speak the language of momentum for a week or two.

But inside the day-to-day machine, the old operating system remains.

Budget owners still submit numbers that reflect last year's beliefs. Forecast conversations still happen too late. Costs still sit in legacy buckets that conceal accountability. Dashboards still report what happened rather than guiding what to do. The FP&A tool still functions like a prettier spreadsheet with the same behavioural dysfunction underneath.

Everyone agreed. No one built.

Three months later, the CEO asks why nothing feels different. The board asks where the execution lift is. Department leaders feel "blamed" when their numbers disappoint because they were never properly equipped to own them. Finance feels frustrated because it gave the organisation the "answers" but not the architecture.

This is a predictable outcome of strategy without scaffolding rather than a failure of competence.

And it is why CFOs who can implement are rare and invaluable.

From Strategy to Build Mode

To bring strategy to life, you must shift from abstract alignment to visible, collaborative movement. In other words, you must move from strategy mode into build mode.

Build mode is the practice of turning direction into routines. It is the practice of converting leadership intention into operational reality, through systems, rhythms, governance, and narrative clarity.

At the enterprise level, “build mode” shows up through five orchestration moves.

1. Systematic Budgeting

This is not merely budgeting for the year. It is building a shared budgeting calendar across departments that becomes a cultural rhythm not a finance ritual.

Budgeting becomes powerful when it is experienced not as compliance, but as coordination. A strong budgeting system creates predictable moments where strategic intent meets departmental reality. It tells the organisation: this is when we plan, this is when we challenge, this is when we commit, and this is when we recalibrate.

A budgeting rhythm that belongs only to Finance produces begrudging participation. A budgeting rhythm that is co-owned by leadership produces better decisions because ownership changes the emotional tone of planning.

The Operational CFO designs this rhythm deliberately. They create clarity around timelines, assumptions, scenario expectations, and decision rights. They ensure the organisation understands what matters most this year and what trade-offs leadership is prepared to make.

2. Cost Centre Clarity

This is not just tracking costs. It is redefining how cost flows map to accountability, so leaders can see what they own and what they influence.

When cost centres are misaligned with operational reality, reporting becomes a mirror that distorts. Leaders see numbers that do not represent their choices. They stop trusting the reports. They become defensive in variance conversations. They treat finance as policing rather than partnership.

Cost centre clarity is, therefore, not an accounting clean-up. It is an accountability reset.

The Operational CFO ensures every cost has a home that makes sense, every manager understands what sits inside their scope, and every cross-functional cost has a visible logic rather than hidden allocation. When cost centre logic becomes comprehensible, leaders begin to manage costs with intelligence rather than reaction.

3. Systems Integration

This is not just adopting a new FP&A tool. It is integrating it into your planning rhythm with training, usage clarity, and phased implementation that fits your organisation's maturity.

Systems fail when they are treated as procurement events rather than behavioural shifts. A new tool does not create better forecasting unless it changes the rhythm of forecasting. It does not create better decisions unless the organisation learns how to interpret, challenge, and act on the outputs.

The Operational CFO leads systems integration as a change programme, not a technology deployment. They ensure the tool supports the planning cadence, not disrupts it. They set adoption expectations and make the system useful for the people who are not finance specialists because enterprise adoption is what converts a finance tool into a decision platform.

4. Dashboards That Drive Decisions

This is not just reporting. It is building living dashboards that guide team priorities, variance management, and performance conversations.

Most dashboards are built to display information. Dashboards are built to drive action. They are designed around decisions: What must we notice early? What requires escalation? What trend changes our behaviour before it becomes a crisis?

The Operational CFO understands that a dashboard is not a visual. It is a discipline. It becomes powerful when it is embedded into leadership conversations, weekly, monthly, quarterly and when the organisation can rely on it as a shared view of reality (Kaplan and Norton, 1996).

5. Transformation Programme Leadership

This is not just influencing. It is managing change through clear timelines, stakeholder maps, governance rhythm, escalation paths, and execution clarity.

Finance transformation fails when it is treated as an extra task layered onto an already full operational agenda. CFOs who execute well recognise that transformation must be managed like a programme: resourced, governed, paced, and protected from scope drift.

Finance becomes the steady hand across departments because it holds the cadence. It tracks what was promised, what is blocked, and what requires decision. It escalates early and resolves without drama. It makes progress visible.

This fifth move is developed explicitly in Chapter 5, where project governance becomes change leadership: stakeholder mapping, adoption rhythms, escalation, communications, and the disciplined management of the messy middle between launch and embedded behaviour.

This is what operational CFO leadership looks like: the ability to coordinate movement without creating chaos.

Why Strategy Fails Without Execution

Here's what I've seen repeatedly across companies of all sizes:

A brilliant strategy was announced. The CEO was excited. Finance was ready.

But implementation lived in a spreadsheet... and never became real.

Why?

Because budgets didn't align with department calendars. The system migration was rushed without data reconciliation. Training never reached the people using the tools. KPIs were set but never translated into dashboards. Cost centre structures were updated in Finance... but not understood in HR or Operations.

The idea was strong. The execution was invisible.

And invisibility is lethal to transformation.

When execution is invisible, leaders stop believing the change is happening. When belief fades, attention shifts. When attention shifts, momentum dies. And when momentum dies, the organisation quietly returns to the old system not because it was better, but because it was familiar.

This is why operational transformation must be treated as executive work. It is not beneath strategy. It is what makes strategy survivable.

The CFO's Dilemma: Precision vs Movement

One of the hardest tensions in execution is this: CFOs are trained to seek precision, but transformation requires movement before perfection.

If you wait for perfect data before migrating a system, you may miss the strategic window. If you insist on flawless cost centre design before changing accountability, you may delay adoption until the organisation is fatigued. If you attempt to build dashboards that answer every question, you will create noise instead of clarity.

Execution leadership is the art of sequencing. You must decide what must be perfect, what must be sufficient, and what can evolve.

CFOs create confidence not by guaranteeing perfection, but by demonstrating control of the process. They build systems that can correct. They create governance that can adapt. They communicate in a way that stabilises the organisation while the build is still unfolding.

What This Book Will Help You Do

By the end of this volume, you will have the frameworks and templates to lead execution with authority without losing the human core that makes adoption possible.

You will be able to lead the annual budgeting cycle across departments with clarity and rhythm, turning the process into a shared organisational cadence rather than a seasonal panic.

You will be able to transition to a new cost centre structure with cross-functional buy-in, ensuring accountability is understood rather than imposed.

You will be able to implement a new FP&A system with proper training and operational alignment, so the tool becomes a decision platform instead of an unused dashboard.

You will be able to build dashboards and reporting tools that create insight and accountability, not just information overload.

And you will be able to guide your leadership team through the messy middle of change without burning out or backing down because you will know how to structure the work, pace the adoption, and keep progress visible.

You will also be able to shape the cost culture around the numbers: creating an environment in which leaders understand the economics of their choices, governance protects speed rather than obstructing it, and accountability remains credible because authority and information travel together.

And when conditions deteriorate, you will be able to orchestrate through crisis without abandoning the system you built. The aim is a finance function that can tighten its cadence, escalate cleanly, preserve decision quality under pressure, and continue to operate with integrity after the current CFO has moved on.

Because being a strategic CFO means more than seeing the future. It means building the systems that carry the company into it.

From Boardroom to Blueprint

Remember: transformation doesn't live in PowerPoint.

It lives in the monthly budget review meeting where Marketing sees their numbers clearly for the first time and realises, they can manage what they can finally understand. It lives in the cost centre training session where team leads stop fearing Finance and start seeing structure as a support, not a threat. It lives in the dashboard login where an operations manager notices a trend before it becomes a problem because the information arrives early enough to matter.

It lives in the FP&A tool adoption where Finance becomes a partner, not a bottleneck because the system was built around decision-making, not around Finance preferences alone.

The work is rarely glamorous, yet it is the work from which legacy is built.

Because when you build infrastructure that makes clarity repeatable, you are not just improving performance this quarter, you are increasing the organisation's capacity to make better decisions long after the current transformation is complete.

Final Thought

Every strategy needs a builder.

Every insight needs infrastructure.

As a CFO, you are no longer just a guardian of financial health, you are now its chief architect. You are not only responsible for what the numbers say, but for whether the organisation can trust them, use them, and act on them.

Let's roll up our sleeves.
Let's orchestrate the system.
Let's make leadership operational.

Chapter 2: Designing the Annual Budgeting Cycle

Tools and templates for budgeting are consolidated in Appendix A – Budget Orchestration Toolkit.

Turning Planning Into a Shared Organisational Rhythm

Every organisation has a budget. But not every organisation has a budgeting rhythm, one that aligns teams, decisions, and timelines into a coordinated flow. Many still treat budgeting as a seasonal administrative event: a rush of templates, a battle of assumptions, a negotiation disguised as planning, and a final number set that becomes outdated before the second quarter is finished.

For the Strategic CFO, budgeting is no longer just about numbers in a spreadsheet. It is about designing an annual operating cadence that drives visibility, accountability, and intelligent decision-making across the enterprise. It is the moment where strategy is translated into constraints and commitments, and where leadership discovers whether it is truly aligned, or merely polite.

This chapter is your blueprint for leading that cycle not as a finance task, but as an organisational discipline: a recurring rhythm that builds shared understanding, surfaces trade-offs early, and gives the business a stable cadence through which it can adjust without chaos. A well-designed budgeting cycle does more than allocate cost. It creates clarity about what matters, who owns what, and when decisions must be made. It turns performance into a shared language rather than a monthly surprise.

The Goal: Alignment, Not Just Approval

Traditional budgeting often looks like this: Finance sends templates. Department heads fill them with hopeful guesses. Numbers are tweaked, defended, reduced. A final version is approved. And by Q2, it is already irrelevant.

What is missing is rarely technical. What is missing is dialogue, purpose, flexibility, and ownership. The organisation has not agreed on the story behind the numbers, the assumptions that hold the plan together, or the rules that determine what happens when reality shifts.

Your job as CFO is not simply to get a budget approved. Your job is to build a budgeting process that enables departments to take ownership of their plans, connects financial data to strategic intent rather than last year's baseline, and embeds adaptability without collapsing into constant renegotiation.

Think of the budgeting cycle as an annual leadership rehearsal. It is the moment the organisation practises how it will lead: what it prioritises, what it protects, what it is willing to trade, and how it behaves when resources are constrained. A budget that is approved but not believed becomes a document people work around. A budget that is believed becomes a rhythm people manage through.

Executive Case Insight: When Budgeting Becomes Theatre

In many organisations, budgeting season feels like a performance. Teams submit inflated numbers because they expect cuts. Risk is hidden in vague lines because uncertainty feels punishable. Leaders defend spend not because it creates value, but because they believe the process is political.

Finance, in turn, tightens controls. It challenges aggressively. It demands detail and tries to force precision out of a context that is inherently uncertain. The result is not alignment. The result is fatigue.

When budgeting becomes theatre, the organisation stops using it as a decision tool. It becomes a compliance ritual. And when it becomes compliance, strategy cannot be executed with speed, because the organisation has not built a shared agreement about what must be funded, what must be constrained, and what trade-offs leadership is willing to accept.

The Strategic CFO breaks this pattern by redesigning the cycle, the process itself produces trust: trust in the assumptions, trust in the trade-offs, and trust in the rules for adjustment. Not trust in Finance as an authority, but trust in the plan as a coherent shared contract.

Step 1: Design the Budget Calendar as a Governance Tool

The first orchestration move is a clear, visible budget calendar. This turns budgeting from a scramble into a staged sequence of decisions. A budget calendar functions as a governance tool as well as a timeline. It tells the enterprise: this is when we align, this is when we challenge, this is when we commit, and this is when we revisit.

A robust annual cycle typically includes five decision movements. First, strategic pre-alignment: the CEO and executive team confirm the enterprise thesis for the year, growth posture, margin expectations, investment priorities, and risk constraints. Second, guidance and assumptions: Finance issues an executive brief that translates strategy into planning parameters. Third, departmental planning: leaders build their plans using drivers and narratives, not just line items. Fourth, calibration: top-down ambition meets bottom-up reality and leadership chooses trade-offs. Fifth, launch and embedding: the budget becomes the baseline for dashboards, reviews, and forecast cadence.

The calendar must reflect operational reality. If Operations is in peak season in October, an October submission deadline is not disciplined, it is unrealistic.

If Sales planning occurs in September, revenue assumptions cannot be set in late November and still be called aligned.

Build buffer time for iteration. Misunderstood assumptions, interdependencies, and executive disagreement are normal. If you do not design rework cycles, you will manufacture panic, and panic manufactures politics.

Most importantly, design around decision moments, not submission moments. Many calendars are built around when Finance needs inputs. Executive calendars are built around when the organisation must decide on headcount, on investment gating, on pricing posture, on cost containment thresholds, and on contingency reserves.

Step 2: Issue a Budget Narrative Pack, Not a Template Email

Budget guidance is where many CFOs unintentionally lose credibility. A spreadsheet template without narrative becomes a vacuum, and vacuums get filled with assumptions, fear, and negotiation. The guidance package must read like an executive brief: short, clear, and anchored to strategy.

A Budget Narrative Pack is a simple but powerful upgrade. It does two things at once. It standardises planning assumptions, departments are not building incompatible versions of reality. And it gives leaders language for explaining their budgets in business terms, not finance jargon.

At minimum, your narrative pack should establish five elements.

First, the enterprise thesis. What is the strategic posture for the year: protect, stabilise, invest, accelerate? What are the headline outcomes (growth, margin, cash, customer, capability)? This is the 'why' that turns budgeting into purpose rather than compliance.

Second, the assumption spine. Provide the parameters that must be shared: inflation, wage growth, FX, pricing assumptions, volume outlook, productivity expectations, and any board constraints. If assumptions are not explicit, debates become emotional rather than analytical.

Third, the non-negotiables. These are the integrity constraints: cash floor, covenant headroom, regulatory commitments, minimum staffing for safety or delivery, and any protected capabilities. The organisation must know what cannot be traded without escalation.

Fourth, the trade zones. Where does leadership invite choice? For example: investment prioritisation within a fixed envelope; reallocations between spend categories; timing shifts between quarters; variable cost levers. Trade zones create ownership because leaders can act, not just comply.

Fifth, the narrative format. Require each leader to submit not only numbers, but a short narrative that answers: what are you trying to achieve, what drivers create the result, what risks could derail it, and what you would do if conditions tightened. When the narrative is standardised, calibration becomes faster because leaders are speaking a shared planning language.

This is what separates budgeting from forecasting. Forecasting tells you what might happen. A budget narrative tells you what the organisation intends to do, and how it will respond when reality deviates from intention.

Board-Grade Budget Narrative: What Must Be Unmistakable

Boards do not need more detail. They need more clarity. A board-grade budget narrative makes three things unmistakable: the strategic posture for the year, the risk boundaries the organisation will not cross, and the decision logic behind major allocations.

If the board cannot see the thesis, it cannot govern. If it cannot see the boundaries, it cannot protect. If it cannot see the logic, it cannot trust. This is why the narrative pack matters: it converts the budget from a pile of figures into a governable plan.

A board narrative should articulate: the enterprise 'north star' metrics (for example, revenue, margin, cash conversion, and liquidity floor); the investment portfolio (what is being funded to create future advantage); the protection plan (what will be tightened first if conditions deteriorate); and the trigger points that would require leadership to return to the board for approval.

Notice what is absent: line-item debate. The board should not be asked to adjudicate whether a department's travel budget is reasonable. It should be asked to endorse the year's posture, the capital allocation logic, and the integrity of the process that produced the plan.

A CFO move is to present the budget as a set of governing questions: What are we choosing to bet on this year? What are we choosing not to do? What risks could break the plan? What early signals will tell us we are entering a tighter regime? What decisions will leadership make automatically, and which ones will return to the board?

When the budget is framed this way, board engagement rises and political budgeting falls, because the organisation knows that allocations are rooted in a thesis, not in influence.

Leader-Grade Budget Narrative: What Executives Need to Run the Year

The executive team requires a different cut of the narrative. Leaders need operationally legible drivers, not only outcomes. They need to understand where performance is expected to come from, which levers they truly own, and what 'good' looks like week-to-week, not just at year-end.

This is where the Budget Narrative Pack becomes a management instrument. It creates a shared language for performance and a shared method for escalation. It reduces the number of meetings spent arguing about whose numbers are correct, because the organisation has agreed on the model spine and the definitions that sit beneath it.

A leader-grade narrative answers: What are our top five performance drivers this year? What decisions will we make if those drivers move outside their expected bands? What resources are protected because they preserve long-term capability? What costs are deliberately variable because we may need flexibility? And what is the cadence for reviewing, reforecasting, and re-authorising investment?

The Budget Narrative Pack in Practice

To make the narrative pack usable, translate it into a small set of repeatable artefacts. These are not 'nice to have' documents. They are the minimum set that makes the budget coherent at board level, runnable at leadership level, and legible at departmental level.

First, the Budget Thesis Memo: a one-to-two-page narrative that summarises the year's posture, major choices, constraints, and risks. This becomes the reference point when conversations drift.

Second, the Assumption Spine: a single source of planning parameters with ownership, refresh timing, and escalation rules. When assumptions are scattered across emails, calibration becomes debate by fatigue.

Third, the Investment Portfolio View: a clear grouping of major initiatives with timing, expected outcomes, and gating logic. This is where strategy becomes visible in the numbers.

Fourth, the Driver Summary: the small set of primary drivers the enterprise will manage through, plus the levers each executive owns. This keeps monthly reviews disciplined and prevents dashboard sprawl.

Fifth, the Contingency and Trigger Sheet: a simple articulation of what tightens first, what is protected, and what thresholds move the organisation from benign to tight. It prevents panic decisions and makes crisis responses pre-agreed rather than improvised.

When these artefacts exist, the budgeting process stops being an annual event and becomes an operating framework that leadership can use every month.

The Executive Budget Story Arc

To keep narrative sharp, structure it as an arc rather than a list. Start with context: what market conditions and operating realities shape the year. Move to choices: what you will prioritise and what you will not. Then commitments: the outcomes and capabilities the budget is funding. Then consequences: what the plan assumes will be true, and what breaks if those assumptions fail. Finally, contingencies: what you will do if the organisation enters a tighter regime.

This arc becomes the CFO's language at every level: leadership calibration, board approval, manager briefings, and monthly reviews. When the story remains consistent, confidence rises, because people can see that the organisation is not improvising, it is navigating.

Step 3: Adopt a Driver-Based Budgeting Doctrine

The fastest way to upgrade budgeting quality is to move from line-item budgeting to driver-based budgeting. Line-item budgeting asks, "What will we spend?" Driver-based budgeting asks, "What will happen in the business that causes spend and performance?" The difference is operational intelligence.

Driver-based budgeting is not complicated. It is disciplined. It forces the organisation to link resources to the realities that produce results: volume, utilisation, capacity, conversion, churn, cycle time, productivity, and service levels.

Begin with a rule: every meaningful budget line must have a driver or a rationale for why it is fixed. If a line cannot be explained through a driver, it becomes a negotiation line. Negotiation lines attract politics.

Drivers differ by function, so the doctrine must be flexible. Revenue drivers may include pipeline volume, conversion rates, average deal size, retention, price/mix, and sales capacity. Operations drivers may include production volume, yield, scrap rates, utilisation, overtime, lead times, and supplier terms. People cost drivers may include headcount, grade mix, attrition, time-to-hire, and learning hours. Technology drivers may include user counts, infrastructure utilisation, licence tiers, and delivery velocity.

The CFO's job is not to dictate drivers. It is to curate a driver library the organisation agrees is legitimate. That library becomes a shared model spine for budgeting and forecasting alike.

Driver Trees: Turning Complexity Into an Executive Model Spine

Driver-based budgeting becomes truly powerful when it is expressed as a driver tree, a simple map that shows how a small set of operational realities flows through to financial outcomes. The tree is not a technical diagram for analysts. It is a leadership device: it teaches executives what to manage, what to watch, and what changes the outcome.

A driver tree begins with the outcome you care about, revenue, gross margin, contribution, EBITDA, cash conversion, and works backwards to the few operational variables that meaningfully move it. If you cannot trace an outcome back to controllable drivers, leaders will treat the result as luck. If you can, leaders begin to manage through levers rather than commentary.

Consider a recurring-revenue business. Revenue is driven by starting customers, new bookings, churn, expansion, and price. Margin is influenced by support effort, cloud costs, licence tiers, and product mix. Cash is influenced by billing terms, collections, and prepayments. When these drivers are explicit, the budget discussion shifts from 'Can we hit the number?' to 'What must be true in conversion, churn, and pricing to hit the number, and what actions will we take if they move?'

Consider a volume-based operations environment. Revenue is driven by volume and price/mix. Cost is driven by capacity, utilisation, labour productivity, yield, scrap, and supplier terms. Cash is driven by inventory turns, procurement timing, and payables policy. The driver tree makes it obvious which improvements create margin, and which merely move cost around without changing economics.

The CFO does not need to build driver trees for every line. Build them for what is material and volatile. A good rule is this: if an item is both large and unpredictable, it deserves a driver tree. If it is small or stable, a simpler treatment is fine. Executive attention is a scarce resource; your models should respect that scarcity.

Driver trees also create a shared language between Finance and functions. Operations leaders can see their world in the financial model without feeling that Finance is imposing abstraction. Commercial leaders can see how pipeline behaviour becomes forecast outcomes. HR leaders can see how hiring pace and attrition flow into capacity and cost. That shared language is what turns budgeting into organisational alignment.

When driver trees are in place, they become the foundation for scenario planning. Each scenario is not a new spreadsheet. It is simply a different set of driver assumptions applied to the same tree. That is how you create speed under uncertainty without sacrificing integrity.

Driver Governance: Definitions, Ownership, and Refresh Cadence

A driver model is only as reliable as the controls around it. If drivers are ambiguous, the model becomes a debate. If driver definitions drift, the organisation loses comparability. If driver ownership is unclear, updates become slow and political.

Define each primary driver with precision: what it is, how it is calculated, what data source is authoritative, and what frequency it is refreshed. Then assign an owner: not necessarily Finance, but the function closest to the operational truth. Finance's role is to curate, validate, and reconcile, to ensure the driver spine remains coherent across the enterprise.

Set a refresh rhythm aligned to volatility. Some drivers deserve weekly review (pipeline conversion, cash collections, utilisation). Some are monthly (headcount, churn, procurement pricing). Some are quarterly (strategic initiatives, structural cost changes). This rhythm becomes the backbone of your performance cycle and prevents reactive reporting.

Finally, establish reconciliation rules. When a driver outcome does not match lived reality, the organisation needs a method for resolving the discrepancy without blame. The question is not, 'Who is wrong?' The question is, 'Which definition, source, or process is drifting, and how do we restore integrity?' That is governance through maturity.

The Build Sequence: Drivers → Capacity → Cost → Cash

Driver-based budgeting works best when built in a deliberate sequence. Start with the drivers: volumes, customers, utilisation, cycle times, conversion, churn. Then translate drivers into capacity: how many people, hours, machines, or seats are required to deliver. Then translate capacity into cost: labour, suppliers, licences, overheads. Finally, translate the plan into cash: working capital, billing terms, capex timing, and liquidity impact.

This sequence is a strategic advantage. It prevents the common failure where organisations budget costs first and only later discover the plan cannot be delivered with the capacity funded. It also elevates the CFO conversation: you are no longer debating whether a cost line is high; you are debating whether the capacity is sufficient to deliver the outcomes, and what trade-offs leadership is willing to make.

From Drivers to Levers

A driver explains causality. A lever is what leadership can change. Budgeting distinguishes between the two. You do not want a budget built on variables leadership cannot influence, because that produces blame without control.

For each function, identify a small set of primary drivers (the 3–7 variables that explain most of the variance) and a set of secondary drivers (useful detail, but not leadership-critical). Then define levers: what can be adjusted mid-year if conditions tighten or opportunities accelerate. Levers might include hiring pace, discretionary spend timing, contractor mix, marketing channel mix, inventory policy, pricing initiatives, or project sequencing.

When drivers and levers are explicit, you can calibrate plans without humiliating teams. You are no longer asking for arbitrary cuts; you are asking leaders to adjust levers while protecting outcomes. That is a different conversation, one that serious executives respect.

Driver Refactoring: Upgrading the Budget Model Without Rebuilding Everything

Most organisations cannot jump from spreadsheet line items to perfect driver models in one cycle. The strategic move is refactoring upgrading the budget model in layers. Start by identifying where line items are already driven implicitly (for example, travel linked to customer visits, or contractor spend linked to project volume) and make those drivers explicit.

Then convert the most volatile and most material areas first. Volatility drives forecast error; materiality drives executive attention. If revenue is volatile, refactor the revenue model. If labour cost is the largest cost base, refactor headcount and productivity. If supply costs swing, refactor procurement and price/mix. This sequencing builds capability without overwhelming the organisation.

Finally, set a standard: each quarter, improve one section of the model. Over time, budgeting becomes less negotiation and more management science. That is how finance functions are built, through consistent doctrine, not one-off transformation programmes.

Step 4: Reconcile Bottom-Up Reality With Top-Down Ambition

Top-down targets are necessary. They are driven by strategy, growth expectations, margin requirements, and board constraints. Without top-down direction, budgeting becomes a collection of departmental wishes.

Bottom-up planning is also necessary. It reflects operational reality: what departments believe is feasible, what resources are required, and what risks are already visible at the front line. Without bottom-up reality, budgeting becomes fantasy.

The reconciliation phase is where CFO sophistication is felt. This is the moment ambition meets constraint, and leadership chooses trade-offs with clarity rather than politics.

Design calibration workshops as decision forums, not line-item battles. Finance does not 'win' by reducing every request. Finance wins by helping leadership see interdependencies, quantify consequences, and choose a coherent plan.

A practical calibration method is to organise discussion by outcomes and capabilities rather than by departments. Instead of 'Marketing versus Finance,' you discuss 'growth efficiency,' 'customer retention,' 'operational capacity,' and 'delivery reliability.' This reduces tribal behaviour and lifts the conversation to enterprise trade-offs.

The Challenge Pack: How to Make Calibration Executive-Grade

Calibration improves dramatically when leaders arrive pre-aligned on facts. Create a simple challenge pack as a pre-read: the latest forecast baseline, the key driver assumptions by function, the top ten variances versus prior year, the top ten investment requests, and the top ten risks that could break the plan.

Then structure discussion around decisions, not explanations. If a leader is requesting incremental headcount, the discussion is framed as capacity and outcomes: What outcome requires this capacity? What will not be delivered without it? What lever could substitute for it (automation, prioritisation, sequencing)? What is the cash and margin impact? This forces trade-offs into the open without turning the room into a defence exercise.

Use redlines intelligently. A redline is not a 'cut'. It is a provisional adjustment that signals, 'This item requires either stronger logic, a better driver link, or an explicit trade-off elsewhere.' Redlines create speed because they compress iteration. They also teach leaders what Finance considers a credible plan.

Finally, close calibration with explicit commitments: the chosen scenario, the protected capabilities, the variable levers, and the triggers that cause revisit. Without this closure, calibration becomes a series of conversations rather than a decision mechanism.

Require each leader to bring three elements: a base plan built on agreed drivers, a protection plan that can be activated if conditions tighten, and an acceleration plan for high-confidence opportunities. When leaders arrive with options, calibration becomes orchestration rather than conflict.

The Budget Decision Log

One of the most underused executive tools in budgeting is a decision log: a simple record of what was decided, why, what assumptions it relies on, and what trigger would cause revisit. This prevents the most common mid-year dysfunction: leaders forgetting the trade-offs they agreed to and reopening debates as if they are new.

A decision log does not need to be complex. It is an integrity instrument. It protects the plan from revisionism and gives Finance a fair basis for saying, 'We can revisit, but here is what must be true for that revisit to be justified.'

Step 5: Build Budget Guardrails That Prevent Chaos Without Killing Agility

Budgeting is not rigid. It is governed. The difference matters.

Contingency Reserves: Funding Flexibility Without Weakening Discipline

A disciplined budget is not the same as a brittle budget. The organisations that navigate uncertainty well usually have one quiet advantage: they have designed flexibility into the plan on purpose, rather than improvising it later through mid-year cuts.

This begins with a visible contingency reserve. The reserve is not 'extra money'. It is a deliberate buffer held against uncertainty, released only through defined governance. It can sit centrally under the CFO or be embedded as small reserves within functions, but it must be governed so it does not become a hidden slush fund.

Pair the reserve with a variable cost architecture. Not every cost should be treated the same under stress. Classify spend into three categories: protected (capability and integrity costs that keep the organisation safe and viable), adjustable (spend that can be slowed or sequenced without breaking delivery), and discretionary (spend that can be paused quickly with minimal strategic damage). When these categories are explicit, shifting regimes becomes a managed transition, not a panic reaction.

The effect is immediate: leaders stop lobbying for 'just in case' buffers inside their budgets, because the enterprise has acknowledged uncertainty openly and built a fair mechanism for absorbing it.

Guardrails are the rules that keep the organisation coherent when reality changes. They define what can be adjusted locally, what requires escalation, what triggers a reforecast, and what thresholds create a shift in operating posture.

Establish a materiality doctrine: what size of variance or commitment change requires CFO review, and what size requires executive team review. Establish reopen rules: under what conditions can a budget be reopened, and who has the authority to approve the reopening. Establish contingency policy: where reserves sit, who can deploy them, and how they are replenished.

These rules are not bureaucracy. They protect speed. Without guardrails, every variance becomes a negotiation, and the organisation burns time debating rather than acting.

A particularly powerful concept is regime thinking benign versus tight. In benign conditions, decision rights can be more decentralised. In tight conditions, decision rights tighten around cash and critical trade-offs. Your budget should define what changes when the organisation shifts regimes. This prevents panic tightening and creates disciplined transitions.

Step 6: Operationalise the Budget as a Living Decision Instrument

Once the budget is approved, many organisations forget it. They load it into systems, distribute a final deck, and move on. The budget becomes a static artefact, useful only for variance discussions that arrive too late to influence behaviour.

Do not let that happen. A budget's power is not in its approval. Its power is in its use.

Operationalise the budget through three mechanisms.

First, integrate it into reporting and dashboards so plan versus actuals is visible in the same view, not reconciled manually by Finance every month.

Second, embed it into leadership rhythms: weekly tactical reviews for leading indicators, monthly performance reviews for drivers and corrective actions, and quarterly reforecasts for scenario updates.

Third, make it a resource allocation language: investment requests, headcount approvals, and project sequencing should reference budget envelopes and decision log commitments.

In organisations, the budget is the annual commitment. The forecast is the updated view of reality. The CFO leads both. The budget anchors discipline; the forecast anchors truth (Hope and Fraser, 2003).

Forecasting Without Budget Collapse

A common fear among executives is that rolling forecasts will undermine the budget. They worry forecasting becomes permission to renegotiate commitments. This is a governance failure, not a forecasting failure.

Make the distinction explicit. The budget is the agreed allocation and performance commitment. The forecast is the updated view of what will happen if current conditions persist. Forecasting does not change commitments automatically. Forecasting changes attention, actions, and escalation.

When the budget is treated as sacred and reality is ignored, leadership becomes fragile. When the budget is treated as disposable and forecasting becomes constant renegotiation, discipline disappears. The Strategic CFO holds the middle path: stable commitments, agile interpretation, and clear rules for when commitments can be revisited.

Step 7: Close the Loop With a Budget Launch That Creates Ownership

The final orchestration step is internal launch and narrative framing. Communicate the budget not as, 'Here is what you are allowed to spend,' but as, 'Here is the plan we built together to move us forward, and here is how we will manage it in real time.'

Tone matters. If the launch feels like restriction, leaders behave defensively. If it feels like direction, leaders behave with clarity. Your launch should restate the enterprise thesis, highlight major choices and trade-offs, confirm key assumptions, and clarify governance: who owns which levers, what the review rhythm is, and how escalation works.

A budget launch also includes role clarity. Budget owners should know what sits inside their envelope, what support Finance will provide, how variances will be discussed, and what 'good budget leadership' looks like. When expectations are behavioural as well as financial, execution improves.

Finally, treat the launch as the start of the year's performance conversation, not the end of planning. Hold briefings, walk leaders through driver logic, and invite questions. People support what they help build, and what they understand.

Common Pitfalls

Copy-paste budgeting. Departments submit last year's numbers with an across-the-board adjustment. No drivers, no strategy, no insight. This happens when leaders feel the process is a formality rather than a decision mechanism.

No reconciliation time. You lock in numbers that nobody believes. This produces a budget that is approved but not owned. Without ownership, execution becomes fragile.

Excel as the shadow system. Manual templates create version chaos and hidden errors. More importantly, they reinforce silo behaviour. The problem is not spreadsheets; the problem is fragmented truth.

Too many rounds. Endless iterations turn budgeting into endurance rather than alignment. Define decision moments, enforce timeboxes, and close cycles cleanly.

Lack of narrative. A silent budget is a weak budget. If leaders do not understand why numbers are what they are, they will not defend them, manage them, or use them.

Final Thought

The budget is not just a financial document. It is a mirror of your organisation's priorities, a map for execution, and a litmus test of alignment.

Your role is not simply to enforce numbers, but to lead a process that creates clarity, ownership, and momentum across the company. Done well, budgeting becomes more than an annual exercise. It becomes a disciplined rhythm through which the organisation learns to commit, to adapt, and to act with coherence.

Financial orchestration is not control for its own sake. It is structure in service of execution, and the annual budgeting cycle is one of the most powerful structures you will ever design.

AI-Assisted Baselining: Speed Without Delegating Judgement

Generative AI and machine-learning tools can shorten the mechanical work of budgeting: clustering historical spend, detecting anomalous run-rates, drafting first-pass narratives, identifying driver relationships, and producing alternative baselines for review. Used well, these capabilities give Finance more time for challenge and interpretation rather than replacing either one.

The boundary is sovereignty of judgement. An AI-generated baseline is an input, not an approved plan. Every material assumption still requires an accountable human owner who can explain the source data, the business logic, the uncertainty around the estimate, and the action that follows if the assumption proves wrong. This is consistent with the risk-management emphasis on governance, traceability, and human accountability in the NIST AI Risk Management Framework and ISO/IEC 42001.

Treat AI-assisted budgeting as a controlled analytical layer. Record which tool produced the output, which data it used, which material transformations occurred, and who reviewed the result. Do not allow generated commentary to become a substitute for driver logic. The faster the tool can produce an answer, the more disciplined the organisation must be about proving why that answer is fit for a decision (NIST, 2023; ISO/IEC 42001:2023).

Chapter 3 – Cost Centre Reorganisation

Tools and templates for cost centre transformation are consolidated in Appendix B – Cost Centre Transformation Pack.

Aligning Financial Structure with Operational Reality

You cannot manage what you cannot see.

And too often, finance teams are flying blind, not because the data is missing, but because the cost centre structure is outdated, misaligned, or misunderstood. In those environments, reporting becomes a distorted mirror.

Leaders are shown numbers that do not reflect their decisions, and they are asked to defend variances they did not create. Finance then works harder and harder to reconcile reality in spreadsheets, while operational leaders quietly stop trusting the outputs.

The way your organisation tracks and allocates costs directly shapes decision-making. When cost centres reflect operational reality, they become a powerful instrument. They show where money is consumed, who owns it, and what levers exist to change the outcome. When they do not, cost centres become a source of confusion, conflict, and poor decisions, plus a subtle drain on executive time.

This chapter will help you redesign your cost centre structure to reflect the business you are, and the one you are becoming. Because cost centre redesign is not merely a finance housekeeping exercise. It is a leadership move. It is one of the most practical ways a CFO can strengthen accountability without creating fear, improve decision quality without increasing bureaucracy, and restore trust in the numbers without requiring everyone to become a finance expert.

When done well, cost centre design becomes part of your enterprise operating system. It allows forecasting to be more reliable, dashboards to be more meaningful, and budget conversations to be more strategic, because the organisation is finally seeing itself clearly.

Why Cost Centres Really Matter

At their best, cost centres are not just reporting lines. They provide visibility frameworks, showing where money is consumed and by whom; accountability anchors, linking decisions to those responsible for them; strategic mirrors, reflecting how the business actually functions, not how it is described in a static org chart; and analytical baselines, enabling variance tracking, benchmarking, and trend analysis that leadership can trust.

In other words, cost centres are not just codes. They are the structure through which the organisation experiences responsibility.

This is why poorly designed cost centres create far more damage than most leaders realise. When cost centres are wrong, allocations become inaccurate. Reports become misinterpreted. Department heads become frustrated. Forecasting models break because the underlying structure does not match how costs truly behave.

Then the organisation develops a dangerous habit. It stops believing the numbers.
When belief erodes, accountability erodes with it. Leaders stop using reports as decision tools and start using them as defence mechanisms. Finance becomes the place where reality is "corrected" rather than the place where reality is clarified.

This is not about micromanagement. It is about financial clarity. And financial clarity is what allows leadership to move faster with less noise.

Executive Case Insight: The Report That Started a War

In one organisation, the CFO introduced a new monthly cost report to "increase ownership". The intent was correct. The execution structure was not.

The report assigned significant shared service costs to operational cost centres based on an old allocation model. Those costs had increased, but operational leaders had no control over the levers that drove them. In the monthly review, leaders were asked why their spending was above plan. They defended themselves. They accused other departments of cost dumping. HR argued that payroll allocations were incorrect. Procurement insisted its savings were not reflected. Finance insisted the model was consistent.

Within two months, a cost centre issue had become a trust issue.

What went wrong was not the reporting. What went wrong was the architecture. Cost centres were misaligned with operational influence. Accountability had been assigned without agency. And once you do that, leaders stop participating in cost conversations as owners. They participate as defendants.

The Strategic CFO understands this early: accountability must be designed with legitimacy. Cost centres must reflect operational reality and operational influence, or the system will generate conflict instead of clarity.

The Hidden Work: Taxonomy Is Strategy

Cost centre redesign is often treated as a tidy-up. The real work is taxonomy design.

Taxonomy is the classification system that tells the enterprise what belongs where. It is the structure that makes cost visible, comparable, controllable, and explainable. When the taxonomy is strong, leaders can look at cost and immediately understand three things: what the cost is, who can influence it, and what decision it should inform. When the taxonomy is weak, cost becomes a fog. People argue about definitions, not performance.

A cost centre taxonomy is not just an accounting map. It is an executive map of responsibility.

That is why taxonomy design principles matter. They stop cost centres becoming a mere reflection of history and politics and instead make them an instrument of strategic clarity.

Taxonomy Design Principles: How to Build a Structure Leaders Can Use

There are nine principles that consistently separate useful cost centre structures from expensive confusion.

1) Design for decisions, not for data

The first question is not "How do we code this cost?" The first question is "What decision should this cost inform?"

If the organisation needs to decide on site profitability, cost centres must support a site lens. If the organisation needs to decide on customer segment economics, cost centres must support cost-to-serve. If the organisation needs to decide on product investment, cost centres must separate product spend from general overhead.
A taxonomy that cannot answer the decisions the business must make will always be bypassed.

2) Make influence match accountability

Accountability without influence creates resentment and gaming. Influence without accountability creates drift. The cost centre owner should be accountable for costs they can influence, or for costs they can manage through agreed levers. If a cost sits outside their control, treat it as a governed shared service cost, not as "their" spending.

3) Build a stable spine with flexible branches

Your taxonomy needs a stable core that will not change every time the org chart changes. That stable spine usually reflects enduring elements: business unit, geography, and the major functions required to deliver value.

Then you create flexible branches that can evolve projects, initiatives, campaigns, and temporary cost objects that capture change without rewriting the core structure.

If everything is built into cost centres, the structure becomes fragile. If everything is built outside cost centres, accountability becomes vague. Balance is the design challenge.

4) Prefer interpretability over extreme granularity

More cost centres do not automatically create more control. Excess detail often creates ambiguity, coding errors, and version drift.

A good structure is one a non-finance leader can interpret quickly. Interpretation drives action. If leaders cannot interpret, they will not own.

5) Separate structural costs from variable costs where it matters

Many cost debates are cost-behaviour debates. What is fixed? What is variable? What is discretionary? What is contractual?

Where it supports decisions, encode that separation in the structure. This can be achieved through cost objects, attributes, or distinct cost centre groupings. The aim is to make elasticity visible, because elasticity is what leaders need in both budget and crisis.

6) Design to prevent "dumping grounds"

Every enterprise has costs that do not fit neatly. If the taxonomy does not provide a logical home, the organisation will create unofficial homes. A "miscellaneous" cost centre becomes the hiding place for poor coding and political avoidance.

A mature taxonomy defines rules for exceptions. It includes an escalation path for costs that do not belong anywhere, and it assigns an owner to resolve them. The goal is not perfection. The goal is to keep the structure meaningful.

7) Standardise naming conventions as a governance tool

Naming is not aesthetics. Naming is cognitive clarity.

Consistent naming should allow anyone to decode what a cost centre represents: location, function, business unit, and scope. A disciplined naming convention reduces training burden, reduces coding errors, and reduces the number of disputes that Finance must settle.

When leaders can read the name and understand the scope, trust increases.

8) Encode the "ownership narrative"

Every cost centre should come with a simple ownership narrative: what it exists to represent, what is included, what is excluded, and what decisions it supports.

This narrative does not belong only in Finance documentation. It belongs in the leadership culture. When owners understand the narrative, they stop treating cost centres as administrative burdens and start treating them as stewardship domains.

9) Treat the taxonomy as a living system with change control

Cost centre redesign does not end at go-live. It ends when the organisation uses the new taxonomy without friction, and when changes are governed.

A change control process protects integrity. It defines who can request changes, who approves them, when they go live, and how comparability is preserved. Without change control, the taxonomy drifts and trust collapses again.

These principles are not theoretical. They are the difference between a structure that supports leadership and a structure that creates politics.

Step 1: Diagnose the Current Structure

Before you build a new structure, you must understand where the old one fails. Cost centre redesign is not a creative exercise. It is an investigative one.

Start with disciplined questions: Leaders typically ask the same questions: "Do current cost centres match operational reality, or do they mirror a historic org chart?"; "Are costs coded consistently across teams and geographies?"; "Are managers being held accountable for costs they cannot influence?"; "Is Finance manually reclassifying data each month to make reporting usable?"; and "Do budget owners understand what is inside their cost centres, and why?"

Pull three to six months of data and look for friction patterns. Repeated reallocations. Ambiguous coding. Duplicate cost centres. Legacy cost centres no one can explain. "Catch-all" cost centres with mixed categories. These are not just accounting imperfections. They are signals that the taxonomy does not reflect the business.

Then listen. Meet with a small set of leaders across Operations, Commercial, HR, IT, and Shared Services. Ask them what they trust and what they ignore. Ask where cost reports feel unfair. Ask where they cannot see the levers.
You will often discover that the core issue is not "the numbers". The core issue is ownership legitimacy.

A strong diagnosis phase ends with a list of structural failures expressed in decision terms: "Leaders cannot see cost-to-serve by segment"; "Shared service costs are contested monthly"; "Managers are accountable for costs they cannot influence"; "Coding rules differ across regions"; and "Finance must reconcile reality manually, which erodes confidence".

That becomes your redesign mandate.

Step 2: Build the Target Taxonomy

Now you design the structure the organisation can use.

Begin with the stable spine. In most organisations, the spine includes business unit or value stream (what you sell, deliver, or operate); geography (where performance is experienced); and function (what work is done).

Then decide where to represent cross-cutting reality. Some organisations need a product lens. Others need a customer segment lens. Others need a project lens. Do not force every lens into cost centres. Use attributes, cost objects, projects, and tags where it improves flexibility.

A practical executive approach is to answer the question: "Where do we want leaders to argue about choices, not definitions?"
If your taxonomy is correct, meetings become about trade-offs. If your taxonomy is wrong, meetings become about whose cost it is.

Design for a small number of levels that correspond to decision rights. If a cost centre is at a level where no one can act, it will become dead reporting. If a cost centre is at a level where the owner cannot interpret, it will become a burden. Match levels to leadership reality.

Step 3: The Shared Services Problem, and Why It Is Political

Shared services are where cost centre redesign either becomes powerful, or collapses into politics.

Shared services include functions like HR, IT, Finance, Facilities, Legal, Security, Procurement operations, and centralised operations centres. These teams often serve the entire enterprise. Their costs are real, necessary, and often growing. The controversy arises when those costs are allocated in ways leaders do not understand or cannot influence.

This creates a predictable dynamic: shared services feel under pressure and underappreciated, because their work is "overhead"; business unit leaders feel punished, because allocations land on them without agency; Finance becomes the referee, because it owns the allocation model; and monthly reviews become debates about fairness instead of conversations about efficiency.

The solution is not to remove shared services costs. The solution is to govern them as internal products.

Shared Services as Internal Products: The Legitimacy Shift

A mature approach treats shared services as internal products with three elements:

1) A service catalogue:

what services are provided and to whom.

2) Demand drivers:

what behaviour or consumption drives cost.

3) Service levels:

what the enterprise expects, and what it is willing to pay for.

When shared services are governed like products, the politics become manageable because costs become explainable.

For example, IT infrastructure costs can be driven by number of devices, users, storage consumption, or application usage. HR costs can be driven by headcount, hiring volume, learning programmes, or employee relations case load. Facilities can be driven by square metres, occupancy, or site utilisation.

You do not need perfect drivers. You need drivers that leaders recognise as legitimate. Legitimacy reduces conflict and increases collaboration.

Chargeback vs Allocation: A Leadership Choice There is a strategic choice in how you apply shared services costs: In practice, this often looks like pure allocation spreads cost but often lacks behavioural signals and chargeback (or internal billing) creates behavioural feedback but can create friction if overly transactional. Many organisations use a hybrid approach: allocate baseline shared services as a "platform cost", then charge back variable consumption above a threshold.

The CFO's job is not to choose the most complex model. It is to choose the model that creates responsible behaviour without creating resentment.

The test is simple: does the method cause leaders to take sensible actions, or does it cause leaders to dispute the method?
If the method creates disputes, it is not yet mature enough to be a governance tool.

Allocation Governance: Make It Contestable, Not Debatable

The aim is not endless debate. The aim is contestability.

Contestability means leaders can challenge errors and logic through a defined process, without turning every monthly meeting into a political battleground.

A strong allocation governance approach includes a documented driver logic and why it was chosen; a review cadence, typically quarterly or bi-annually; an error correction pathway for mis-coding or unusual events; and a steering decision path for changing drivers, because changing drivers changes power dynamics.

This is shared services politics in its most honest form. Allocation models redistribute perceived responsibility. That is why the governance must be transparent and consistent. Inconsistency creates suspicion. Transparency creates legitimacy.

Step 4: Map the Old to the New, Without Losing Comparability

This step is critical, and where most projects collapse.

Cost centre redesign fails most often not because the new structure is wrong, but because the transition is poorly managed. The organisation loses comparability. Finance loses control of reporting integrity. Leaders lose confidence because historical baselines vanish.

Create a mapping that translates old cost centres to new ones with explicit ownership and logic. Validate it with functional leads. Define how historical reporting will be restated, where it will not, and how trends will be interpreted across the change. Be explicit about what is comparable and what is not.

Then run a shadow cycle before go-live. Do not skip this.

A shadow cycle means you run outputs in parallel: old structure versus new structure. You compare differences. You identify logic gaps and coding issues. You test whether leaders interpret the new view correctly. You resolve confusion before it reaches executive forums.

This is how you protect trust.

Step 5: Assign Ownership That Works in Practice

Every cost centre must have a named owner; a defined scope (included and excluded costs); and a Finance partner to support interpretation and coaching.

Ownership is not only administrative. It is psychological. When a leader is named as an owner, the organisation signals stewardship. The leader begins to see patterns, ask better questions, and participate in trade-offs.

However, ownership without support becomes abandonment. Many leaders do not know how to read cost centre views with confidence. This is where Finance must mature from reporting to coaching. Your Finance partners should help budget owners interpret drivers, understand allocations, and distinguish between controllable and uncontrollable variances.

Cost centre redesign is also an opportunity to improve financial literacy across the enterprise. You are not simply giving leaders new codes. You are giving them a new mirror. Teach them how to read it.

Step 6: Build the Change Governance, or the Taxonomy Will Drift

A redesigned structure can still fail after launch if governance is weak. The taxonomy drifts through informal changes, new teams, reorganisations, and local exceptions.

Define a cost centre change control process: who can request a new cost centre and why; what evidence is required (decision need, ownership, expected lifespan); who approves the request (usually Finance governance with business confirmation); when it goes live (monthly cutovers reduce chaos); how naming and hierarchy rules are applied; and how historical comparability is preserved.

Also define a reclassification policy. Reclassification should be allowed but disciplined. If reclassifications happen casually, leaders lose confidence. If reclassifications are forbidden, mistakes accumulate. The policy must define what can be corrected, by whom, and within what timeframe.

Finally, define how exceptions are handled. Every taxonomy needs an exception mechanism that protects integrity without creating a permanent dumping ground.

The CFO's Discipline: Create Psychological Safety for Cost Truth

Cost ownership fails when leaders fear punishment. If every variance conversation feels like an interrogation, leaders will hide. They will delay escalations. They will manipulate coding. They will protect their narratives rather than reveal reality (Edmondson, 1999; 2019).

A mature cost centre system creates emotional safety for truth, while maintaining discipline for action.

You create that safety by separating explanation from blame; normalising early escalation by rewarding leaders who raise risks early; making shared service allocations transparent so leaders do not feel ambushed; using consistent rules so leaders trust the system is fair; and avoiding performative "savings targets" that ignore operational reality.

This is not softness. This is control through trust. When leaders feel safe to tell the truth, Finance gets better information earlier. That improves forecasting, reduces surprise, and improves cost outcomes.

Shared Services Politics, Continued: The Coalition You Must Build

Because shared services costs sit across the enterprise, redesigning them requires coalition work. It is not enough to build a model. You must build agreement.

A practical executive approach is to host a shared services alignment workshop with three outputs:

1) Shared definition of services and service levels.

2) Agreement on the cost drivers that feel legitimate.

3) Agreement on what decisions the allocation model should enable.

Finance should not position itself as the judge of fairness. Finance should position itself as the designer of a system that makes fairness discussable and efficiency achievable.

When shared service leaders are involved, they also gain discipline. They become accountable not only for their cost base, but for their unit economics and service commitments. When business unit leaders are involved, they gain agency. They can influence demand drivers and request service level adjustments when trade-offs are needed.

This is where cost centre redesign moves from structure to leadership. You are creating a shared language of cost reality.

Step 7: Operationalise the New Structure in Systems and Rhythms

The change will not stick unless it is embedded.

Update ERP, payroll and HR coding, procurement workflows, approval matrices, BI tools, dashboards, budget templates, and forecasting models. Align the chart of accounts and cost centre logic so that the organisation does not experience hybrid reporting, which destroys trust quickly.

Then embed the new structure into the monthly cadence: monthly cost reviews that focus on drivers and actions; quarterly allocation reviews for shared services; forecast updates that use the new structure as the default; and leadership dashboards that reflect the taxonomy consistently.

The most important behavioural moment is when Excel stops being the "real view".

This does not mean banning spreadsheets. It means ending shadow reporting where spreadsheets hold the truth and the ERP holds the presentation. One structure. One source. One narrative.

How to Measure Success After Go-Live

Cost centre redesign should deliver observable outcomes beyond "the chart changed".

Look for: Look for reduction in manual journals and reclassifications; reduction in monthly reporting disputes; faster month-end reporting cycle for management reporting; improved forecast accuracy, because ownership is clearer; increased use of dashboards and cost views by non-finance leaders; and clearer accountability conversations focused on levers, not blame.

You are not measuring bureaucracy. You are measuring usability.

Common Pitfalls

These failures are predictable, and avoidable.

Changing structure without changing ownership. The chart updates, but behaviour does not.

Overcomplicating the hierarchy. Complexity masquerades as control but destroys interpretability.

Ignoring shared services politics. Allocations become a monthly war, and the structure loses legitimacy.

Failing to engage IT, HR, and Procurement early. Cost centres are embedded in systems those functions manage.
Skipping the shadow cycle. Errors become visible in executive forums, which costs trust.

Leaving communication to an email. Rollout requires presence. Leaders need to feel supported, not judged.

Treating taxonomy as "done" at go-live. Without change control, drift will rebuild the same problems.

Taxonomy Blueprint: The Four Cost Domains Leaders Need to See

Most organisations become clearer when the cost centre taxonomy explicitly separates four domains of cost. You can represent these domains in cost centre groupings, in reporting hierarchies, or through attributes, but the principle is the same: leaders need to know which costs are directly tied to delivery and which costs are the enterprise platform.

1) Direct delivery costs

These are costs that move with volume or delivery and are closely tied to how the organisation creates value. In manufacturing this is often plant labour and production support. In services it may be delivery teams, customer success, or client projects. These costs should be visible at the level where operational leaders can pull levers.

2) Business enablement costs

These are costs that support delivery but are not always directly variable, such as local HR partners, local IT support, local finance operations, and operational management layers. These costs often sit in a grey zone and create disputes if not classified carefully. The aim is not to label them as "bad overhead". The aim is to make them transparent so leaders can evaluate what enablement they are buying.

3) Shared services platform costs

These are centralised services that function like internal infrastructure. They are necessary for scale and governance, but they are also the costs that most frequently become political, because they are real yet not felt as controllable. These costs should be governed with service catalogues and demand drivers, otherwise they become "the tax nobody understands".

4) Corporate and strategic investment costs

These include executive leadership, enterprise programmes, compliance, long-term capability investments, and strategic initiatives. They should not be scattered across operational cost centres. When corporate investment is hidden in operational lines, leaders lose their ability to see the true cost of running the enterprise. This domain requires board-level narrative, because it reflects intentional choices about long-term capability.

When these domains are visible, executive conversations become more intelligent. Leaders stop treating all costs as equal. They begin to distinguish between costs that must be optimised, costs that must be governed, and costs that must be intentionally invested.

The Cost Centre "Unit of Accountability": How Far Down Should You Go?

A cost centre should exist at the level where someone can reasonably own the economics and influence the outcome.

If you create cost centres below that level, you create noise. Coding becomes inconsistent, and small variances become distractions. If you create cost centres above that level, you create blindness. Leaders cannot isolate levers, and the organisation loses the ability to understand what is driving variance.

A practical way to decide the right level is to ask three questions: Leaders typically ask the same questions: "If this cost centre is off plan, who will be asked to explain it?"; "What levers do they have to change it within one quarter?"; and "What decisions should this cost centre support at executive level?"

If you cannot answer those questions cleanly, the level is wrong.

Taxonomy Archetypes: Different Businesses Need Different Mirrors

Cost centre structures fail when they are copied from another company without respecting business model reality. There is no universal "best taxonomy". There is only a taxonomy that fits the decisions your business must make.

Three common archetypes illustrate the difference:

1) Multi-site operations

If you operate plants, warehouses, clinics, stores, or distribution sites, site-level visibility is non-negotiable. Leaders must see cost by site, including shared service support, maintenance, local overhead, and capacity. The taxonomy must allow site profitability analysis and enable a "site leader owns site economics" culture.

2) Product and platform businesses

If you build products, the critical lens is product investment. Leaders must see spend by product line, platform, and major programmes. The taxonomy must separate product development from corporate overhead and allow visibility of run versus change spend, because that is where investment decisions live.

3) Project-based services

If you deliver through projects or client work, cost must be seen through project economics and utilisation. Cost centres often represent teams and practices, while projects capture delivery economics. In this model, forcing project economics into cost centres creates distortion. The taxonomy should keep stable team accountability and use projects to capture delivery-level insights.

Shared Services Politics: The Three Conflicts You Must Resolve

Shared services costs become political for three reasons, and each has a different solution.

Conflict 1: "We pay, but we do not choose."

This is an agency problem. Leaders receive allocations but cannot influence the service level or demand driver. The solution is governance: define what is standard, what is premium, and what can be adjusted. Give leaders a way to make service level trade-offs.

Conflict 2: "The model feels arbitrary."

This is a legitimacy problem. Leaders do not recognise the drivers. The solution is transparency and simplicity. Choose drivers leaders understand, even if they are not perfect. Perfect drivers that nobody trusts are useless. Trusted drivers that are directionally fair are powerful.

Conflict 3: "Shared services are treated as overhead, not as work."

This is a respect problem. Shared services become defensive, business units become resentful, and Finance becomes stuck in the middle. The solution is to treat shared services as internal products with defined outcomes and unit costs. When shared services can say "this is what you get for this cost", the conversation shifts from blame to optimisation.

The Two Levers Doctrine: Reduce Demand or Reduce Unit Cost

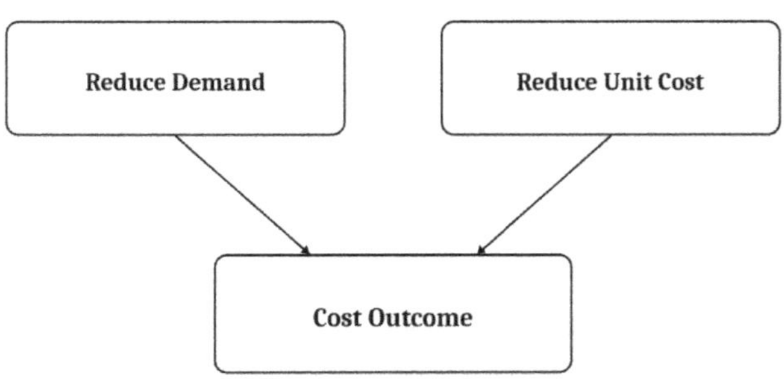

Figure 1 — Two Levers Doctrine

Once shared services are treated as internal products, leaders can use the two levers that matter: reduce demand by changing behaviours, standardising tools, or simplifying processes; and reduce unit cost by improving efficiency, automating, consolidating vendors, or redesigning service delivery.

Without this doctrine, cost conversations stay emotional. With it, they become operational.

Rollout Risk Register: The Executive Version

Every cost centre reorganisation contains risks that should be named upfront, not discovered in the first management review.

The most common risks include comparability loss, where leaders cannot track trend performance across the change; coding drift, where teams interpret rules differently and accuracy declines; shadow reporting, where Excel becomes the "real view" because confidence is not yet earned; allocation backlash, where shared service distributions trigger resentment and political conflict; systems misalignment, where HR, payroll, procurement, or BI tools lag behind the new structure; ownership gaps, where cost centres exist but no one actively manages them; over-design, where complexity creates failure because the organisation cannot adopt it; and under-communication, where leaders experience surprise rather than support.

The purpose of naming risk is not to create caution. It is to create readiness. CFOs lead redesigns as credibility programmes, and credibility is protected through risk discipline.

Design Workshops: How to Build Agreement Without Losing Control

A cost centre redesign cannot be designed in isolation and then announced. If it is, it will be implemented formally and resisted informally.

Run structured workshops with leaders who will own the outcomes. The CFO should set the constraints but invite leaders to shape the structure within those constraints. A simple workshop sequence is:

Workshop 1: Decision lens, what leaders need to see to manage better.

Workshop 2: Ownership lens, who influences what, and where accountability should sit.

Workshop 3: Shared services lens, what services exist, what drivers are legitimate, and what governance is needed.

Workshop 4: Validation lens, test the taxonomy on real data and real scenarios, then refine.

These workshops speed adoption because they build belief. When leaders help build the structure, they defend it.

Final Thought

Cost centres are not just accounting structures. They are how your organisation understands itself. They define what is visible, what is owned, and what is manageable.

When you realign them with purpose, legitimacy, and interpretability, you are not just cleaning up data. You are building a new level of financial ownership and insight across the business. You are giving the enterprise a clearer mirror, and therefore a clearer ability to act.

It is not structure for structure's sake.

It is structure in service of strategy.

And when the structure is right, execution becomes lighter, because clarity becomes shared.

Chapter 4: Transitioning FP&A Systems

Tools and templates for system transition are consolidated in Appendix C – FP&A System Transition Playbook.

Aligning Tools with Vision, Not Just Transactions

Most finance teams don't resist new systems. They resist new systems that feel misaligned, rushed, or irrelevant. They resist being handed a platform that promises transformation but delivers friction. They resist being told that a tool will "save time" when, in practice, it adds steps, creates confusion, and requires them to rebuild trust in every number from scratch.

A successful FP&A system transition is not just a technical upgrade; it is a strategic opportunity. Done well, it enables real-time forecasting, cross-functional alignment, and faster decision-making. Done poorly, it becomes an expensive dashboard no one trusts; a layer executives' glance at and quietly ignore; a "finance initiative" that never becomes an enterprise asset.

This chapter outlines how to lead a system transformation that works operationally, culturally, and strategically. Not as a procurement exercise, but as a leadership programme. The tool will not transform your finance function by itself. Your leadership through the transition is what determines whether the system becomes a decision platform, or an unused interface.

In FP&A transitions, the "system" is never the product. The product is a new decision operating model: faster cycles, clearer drivers, governed definitions, and visible accountability. Your platform should be the infrastructure that makes that operating model possible. The moment your platform starts to shape behaviours, you have begun the real transformation.

Why the System Matters

The FP&A system you use determines how fast you can adapt forecasts, whether departments trust the numbers, whether insight arrives in time to make a difference, and whether Finance is a partner, or a bottleneck. An FP&A tool is not just about automation. It is about enabling strategic visibility at every level of the organisation. It is about creating one shared reality, one version of the truth, that leaders can use to make decisions without waiting for the next monthly close.

When chosen and implemented wisely, a system can materially reduce manual work, enable self-serve access to performance data, standardise scenario planning across departments, and support rolling forecasts and faster reforecasting during volatility. But those outcomes do not come from software alone. They come from redesigned behaviours and rhythms built around the tool (Davenport and Harris, 2007).

It is tempting to assume that technology is the main problem. Most FP&A system failures are behavioural failures dressed up as technical issues. The organisation doesn't trust the inputs, so it doesn't trust the outputs. Leaders don't understand model logic, so they resist using it. Departments don't see the system as relevant to their decisions, so adoption stays superficial. Finance keeps exporting data into spreadsheets "just in case", and the old system quietly survives underneath the new layer.

The Strategic CFO recognises the core truth early: the system is only as powerful as the operating rules built around it. Platforms give capability; governance gives credibility; consistency gives adoption. When those three work together, finance stops being a reporting function and becomes an organisational navigation system.

Four outcomes to design for

To make an FP&A transition credible to CEOs and boards, anchor it around outcomes they care about. The most credible transitions deliver four results consistently and measurably.

First, integrity: the organisation trusts the numbers because definitions are governed and lineage is visible.

Second, speed: the organisation can reforecast fast enough to matter, not just fast enough to report.

Third, explainability: leaders can interpret movement through drivers, not through post-hoc storytelling. Fourth, ownership: accountability sits where decisions sit, not where spreadsheets sit.

When these outcomes are explicit, the system selection, implementation sequence, and adoption governance become easier to justify. You are no longer buying software; you are buying an operating advantage.

Executive Case Insight: The System That Went Live, and Still Didn't Exist

Many organisations experience the same pattern. The system goes live on schedule. The vendor celebrates. The programme team closes the plan. The CFO announces success. And then, quietly, the organisation returns to Excel.

"Go-live" is not the moment the system begins to exist. "Go-live" is the moment the organisation begins to decide whether it believes the system is real. If model outputs are inconsistent, if dashboards refresh too slowly, if cost centre structures don't match operational reality, or if leaders cannot reconcile new reports with their lived experience, the system becomes a glossy layer on top of old habits.

Finance keeps the platform alive for reporting, but the business does not use it for decisions. When the business does not use it, the CFO has not implemented a decision platform; they have implemented a reporting interface. This is why CFOs lead FP&A transitions as credibility projects. Because the real product is not the system. The real product is trust.

Trust is created in three places. It is created in the data pipeline when refresh and reconciliation are consistent. It is created in the model when drivers explain performance in a way leaders recognise. And it is created in executive routines when the platform is used in real meetings, under real pressure, without a spreadsheet escape hatch.

Step 1: Evaluate the Readiness Landscape

Before choosing a platform, assess the readiness landscape. Tool selection without readiness assessment is how organisations buy ambition they cannot operationalise.

Start with strategic fit. Does the tool support rolling forecasts and multi-scenario planning? Can it model cost centre logic, project-based budgeting, and driver-based forecasting? Does it support your future operating model, not just your current reporting needs?

Then assess organisational maturity. Are your teams ready for self-serve dashboards, or do they still depend on Finance to interpret performance? Do leaders understand variance and forecast logic, or do they treat the forecast as a "finance number"? What is the organisation's change fatigue level right now? How much behaviour change can you realistically sustain in the next ninety days?

Next, assess technology and data. Will it integrate cleanly with your ERP, HRIS, CRM, procurement, and billing systems? Where does master data live, who governs it, and how often does it change? How clean are your cost centres, product hierarchies, and customer segment definitions? If you are redesigning cost centres, coordinate that work with the system transition, so you do not rebuild the future on yesterday's structure.

Finally, assess capability. Do you have a planning lead who can translate business questions into model design? Do you have a data owner who can make lineage visible? Do you have change capacity to run training, clinics, and adoption governance? If you do not, your vendor will happily "implement" the system while your organisation quietly fails to absorb it.

A practical readiness diagnostic

Rather than writing a long report, run a short diagnostic across stakeholders. Ask five questions in leadership interviews and listen for patterns.

1) Where do we currently lose time: building the forecast, validating the data, or interpreting the results?

2) What decisions are made too late today, and what would "in time" look like?

3) What are the most contested numbers in the business, and why are they contested?

4) Which managers treat budgets as ownership tools, and which treat them as negotiation documents?

5) What is our tolerance for new process, and what would overwhelm our teams?

Your answer will tell you whether you need a sophisticated platform immediately or a phased capability build. It will also tell you where trust is likely to collapse during transition, and where you must over-invest early.

The CFO's Hidden Decision: Build for the Organisation You Have, or the One You Want?

There is a strategic tension at the heart of system selection. Choose a tool designed for where you are today and you may limit your future capability. Choose a tool designed for where you want to be and you may accelerate transformation or overwhelm the organisation.

The answer is rarely "buy the most advanced product". The answer is to buy a platform that allows you to evolve and to implement in phases that respect current capability. CFOs do not buy transformation and hope for adoption. They buy a platform and orchestrate the adoption path deliberately.

The Platform Selection Scorecard

Boards and CEOs rarely want to hear that a system was chosen because "the demo was impressive". They want to know that selection was disciplined, comparable, and aligned to the operating model. A selection scorecard gives you that rigour and, just as importantly, helps you defend the decision when cost pressures and politics inevitably appear.

A strong scorecard does not pretend that technology choices are objective. It acknowledges judgement and makes judgement visible. It forces trade-offs into the open: integration strength versus user experience; planning sophistication versus simplicity; speed of implementation versus long-term sustainability.

Design the scorecard around decision capability first, not around features. A vendor may offer hundreds of features. Your organisation will use a small set of capabilities repeatedly, under time pressure, with executives watching. Those capabilities should dominate weighting.

Five scorecard dimensions

Decision capability: rolling forecasts, multi-scenario modelling, driver-based planning, and the ability to explain movement without manual adjustment. If the tool cannot support decision speed, it will be a reporting upgrade, not an orchestration platform.

Integration and data pipeline: stability of connectors, refresh cadence, and the ability to trace a KPI from dashboard to source system. If the pipeline is fragile, trust will collapse faster than adoption can build.

Model design and governance: dimensionality without duplication, audit trails, version control, and access controls. If definitions drift and changes cannot be traced, the system will not survive crisis scrutiny.

User experience and workflow: budget owners must complete tasks without finance translation. The interface must reduce effort for the business, not relocate effort into new steps.

Total cost of ownership: licences matter, but so do implementation effort, internal maintenance, training load, and dependence on external consultants. A platform that requires permanent consultants is not a decision asset; it is a recurring liability.

How to use the scorecard like an executive

Treat the scorecard as a decision brief, not a spreadsheet. Keep criteria limited. Weight what matters for your context, not what the vendor markets.

If you are scaling rapidly, prioritise integration reliability and driver-based modelling. If you are in a volatile market, prioritise scenario speed and reforecast cadence. If you have low maturity and high change fatigue, prioritise user experience and phased adoption.

Run three evaluation rounds:

Round one: exclude platforms that cannot meet non-negotiables (integration requirements, multi-entity planning, auditability). This saves time and prevents political drift.

Round two: test a real use case. Take one business unit, one driver model, and one dashboard view. Ask budget owners to perform tasks. Measure friction. Do not accept vendor-led "walkthroughs" as evidence. Require the users who will live inside the tool to touch it.

Round three: stress test governance. Ask how the system handles definition changes, version control, approvals, and access. Ask how it prevents shadow forecasts, and how you will detect when shadow work returns.

When you reach the board, your selection story should be simple: we chose this platform because it strengthens decision speed, protects integrity, and is implementable in our organisation. Anything more complex reads like justification rather than judgement.

Sixth, assess AI readiness. Can the platform distinguish governed model outputs from human-entered assumptions? Can it record model/version provenance, preserve prompt or configuration history where relevant, restrict sensitive data, route material AI-produced outputs for review, and make it clear to executives when a number or narrative has been generated rather than directly sourced? A platform that adds AI without traceability adds speed and ambiguity at the same time.

Step 2: Build a Phased Implementation Plan

Break your rollout into clear stages. Phased implementation is not just project management; it is changing management disguised as sequencing.

Phase 1, Foundation: define planning outcomes, lock core definitions, map data sources, and build the governance spine. Decide what success will be measured by and which behaviours must change. The foundation phase is where you decide what is fixed and what is flexible.

Phase 2, Pilot: test with one function or region. Migrate sample data and run a parallel forecast cycle. The pilot is not about proving the system can work. The pilot is about proving the organisation can work with the system.

Phase 3, Expand: roll out in waves, with weekly clinics and structured feedback loops. Expansion is where adoption becomes cultural. If you rush it, resistance becomes structural. People will comply publicly while reverting privately.

Phase 4, Integrate: build stable pipelines to ERP and adjacent systems. Validate refresh reliability and lineage. Integration is where trust is either won or permanently damaged. This is where you must be ruthless on reliability.

Phase 5, Embed: make the system the default. Decommission legacy templates. Require that executive reviews and reforecasts use the platform. Embedding is when the system becomes real because it stops being optional.

Avoid the "big bang". Go live in waves. Celebrate wins. Fix bugs early. Protect the organisation from feeling the system is being imposed. Adoption must feel like an upgrade to decision-making, not an administrative burden.

The executive rollout artefacts

Transition produces a small set of artefacts that senior leadership recognises as "serious". Not because they are long, but because they are disciplined.

A one-page success definition: what will improve, by when, and how it will be measured. A governance map: who owns definitions, who owns the pipeline, who owns the model. A refresh and reconciliation calendar: when the data updates and how discrepancies are resolved. And a meeting adoption plan: which leadership routines will move into the system and when.

These artefacts transform the transition from a project into a new operating model.

Model Refactoring: From Line Items to Drivers

The most expensive mistake in FP&A transitions is copying old spreadsheet logic into a new platform. If your forecasting model is a patchwork of line-item assumptions, you will simply build faster confusion.

FP&A system transition is a chance to refactor the model. The move is from line items to drivers, from inputs that are arbitrary to inputs that explain performance. Driver-based planning does not mean modelling everything. It means modelling what matters.

Begin with a simple test: if a leader challenges the forecast, can you explain the movement through drivers they recognise? If the answer is no, your model is not a decision model. It is a reporting model.

Selecting drivers with discipline

Drivers should satisfy three criteria. They must be causally linked to outcomes. They must be observable (from systems or reliable operational reporting). And they must be actionable by a named owner.

Revenue drivers may include volume, price, conversion, churn, average order value, and sales cycle duration. Cost drivers may include headcount, utilisation, unit cost, supplier rates, or cost-to-serve by segment. Working capital drivers may include DSO, DPO, inventory turns, and returns.

The executive benefit is interpretability. When leaders can explain a forecast through drivers, they trust it. When they cannot, they argue with it.

A practical driver conversion sequence

First, freeze definitions. What counts as revenue? What counts as acquisition cost? Which costs sit in cost of sales versus operating expenses? If definitions drift, drivers become meaningless.

Second, build a driver library. One page per driver: definition, source system, refresh cadence, owner, and how it flows into the model. This library becomes the backbone of governance and is one of the clearest "signals" you can show a board: the organisation has codified how value is generated and consumed.

Third, simplify the hierarchy. Many finance teams build models that mirror the chart of accounts. That is a reporting mindset, not a planning mindset. Planning models should mirror decision levers. Build views around what leaders can change.

Fourth, create explainability. Build outputs that show what changed and why: volume, price, mix, timing, and productivity. Without explainability, you will still be asked to "send the Excel".

Fifth, design for scenario speed. In volatility, the ability to produce a credible downside scenario in hours is a strategic advantage. Driver models make that possible because you adjust a small set of levers rather than rewriting an entire forecast.

Driver governance under pressure

The first-time markets move; leaders will demand manual overrides. Some overrides will be sensible. Others will be political. Your system must allow judgement without destroying integrity.

Set an override protocol. Require that overrides be labelled, time-bound, and reconciled back into drivers within a defined window. The goal is not to prohibit judgement. The goal is to stop judgement becoming a permanent second model.

Data Lineage and Reconciliation Doctrine

You cannot sustain adoption without trust, and you cannot sustain trust without lineage. Leaders need to know where numbers come from, how they were transformed, and why they can be believed.

Data lineage is the discipline of making the journey visible: from source systems to the planning model to dashboards. Reconciliation is the discipline of proving that journey is correct. The point is executive integrity, not technical obsession. It protects integrity under pressure.

A simple lineage doctrine for CFOs

Every critical KPI has a named owner, a definition, and a source of truth. Every transformation step is documented: what was mapped, aggregated, or adjusted, and why. Every material adjustment is traceable: who changed it, when, and with what approval. And every dashboard can be reconciled back to source reliably and consistently.

Think of lineage as your "audit trail for decisions". When a CEO asks why a KPI moved, you should not need a forensic exercise. You should be able to show the pathway with calm clarity.

The three reconciliations that protect trust

Reconciliation to the general ledger: does the system align with financial truth at close and on interim refreshes? Reconciliation to operational systems: do drivers match CRM, HRIS, and operational realities? And reconciliation to cash: does the planning model produce cash implications that match treasury reality?

Most organisations reconcile only to the ledger and wonder why business leaders do not trust the forecast. Operational reconciliation is often the missing link. If sales leaders see conversion rates that do not match their pipeline, they will discount the entire platform.

Parallel reporting is the trust bridge

Parallel reporting is not wasted effort. It is where leaders learn that the new system is not producing "different numbers", but producing the same truth with more speed, clarity, and usability. Run old and new outputs side by side. Do not hide differences. Differences are signals that help you correct logic and build belief.

When to stop reconciling

Stop when three conditions are true: the refresh rhythm is stable; definitions are locked and governed; and executive meetings use the system without requesting spreadsheet backups. Until then, reconciliation is the cost of credibility.

AI extends lineage rather than escaping it. If a forecast, scenario, anomaly flag, or written commentary is produced by a model, the decision trail should still show the authoritative source data, material transformations, model or service used, review status, and accountable sign-off. The principle is simple: no model-produced number earns executive standing merely because it is plausible. It earns standing when the organisation can trace, challenge, reproduce where appropriate, and govern how it entered the decision process.

This is especially important with copilots and agentic workflows that can retrieve data, transform it, and draft conclusions in one sequence. Convenience can collapse several control points into a single interaction. Finance therefore needs an explicit rule for where human review is mandatory, where automated actions are permitted, and where the system must stop and escalate.

Step 3: Engage Cross-Functional Champions

System transitions fail when Finance owns everything alone. When the tool is perceived as "Finance's system", it will be used by Finance, tolerated by leadership, and ignored by the rest of the organisation.

Identify champions in Sales, Operations, HR, Procurement, Product, and any business unit with meaningful complexity. Involve them early. Let them test, critique, and shape how the tool works for their teams. Give them ownership of specific elements: driver definitions, workflow design, and training inside their functions.

Champions do more than support training. They translate finance logic into functional relevance. They reduce fear because peers trust them. They also surface practical issues early, friction points Finance would not see alone.

Recognise champions publicly. This is cultural change, not just implementation. When champions feel valued, they become ambassadors rather than reluctant participants.

Step 4: Train for Understanding, Not Just Usage

Training fails when it focuses on buttons, not behaviours. People leave knowing where to click but not knowing how to interpret what they see or how it changes the way they lead.

Training should answer three questions: what does this tool help me see; how does this change the way I make decisions; and how do I read a dashboard or variance report with confidence?

Design training by role. Budget owners need workflows and interpretation, not model architecture. Analysts need model discipline, driver governance, and scenario building. Executives need short orientation: how to read the system, what to ask, and what decisions it will accelerate.

Provide clinic support for the first sixty to ninety days. Clinics reduce private frustration and prevent the return of shadow spreadsheets. Most importantly, embed training into leadership routines. If leaders see the system used in executive reviews, they learn its language. If they never see it used at the top, they will assume it is optional.

Adoption Metrics and Behavioural Governance

Most organisations track adoption informally: "people seem to be using it". That is not governance. Adoption must be measured, because adoption is the only indicator that the system is becoming real.

Track adoption through a small set of executive metrics: active usage (target users completing role tasks each cycle); forecast cycle time (request to consolidated forecast); scenario turnaround time (credible downside scenario with driver narrative); reconciliation effort (hours spent and trend); decision utilisation (frequency used in leadership meetings); and model discipline (proportion of changes explained through drivers rather than manual overrides).

These metrics are behavioural, not technical. They tell you whether the organisation is adopting the platform as a decision system, not simply tolerating it as a reporting tool.

Behavioural governance is the rule-set that makes adoption stick

One forecast doctrine: there is one official forecast, and it lives in the platform. Meeting doctrine: executive reviews and variance conversations use the system view, not exported spreadsheets. Reopen rules: forecasts are updated on a defined cadence or on trigger breaches, not on ad hoc lobbying. Ownership doctrine: budget owners own their drivers; Finance owns model integrity; the CFO owns governance. Clinic rhythm: for the first ninety days, run weekly clinics and publish what improved because of feedback.

When governance is explicit, resistance declines. People stop treating the system as something imposed and start treating it as something that protects them from confusion.

The Planning Stack: From Source to Signal

A platform transition is not only a change of interface. It is an opportunity to modernise the full planning stack, the architecture that turns transactions into executive signals.

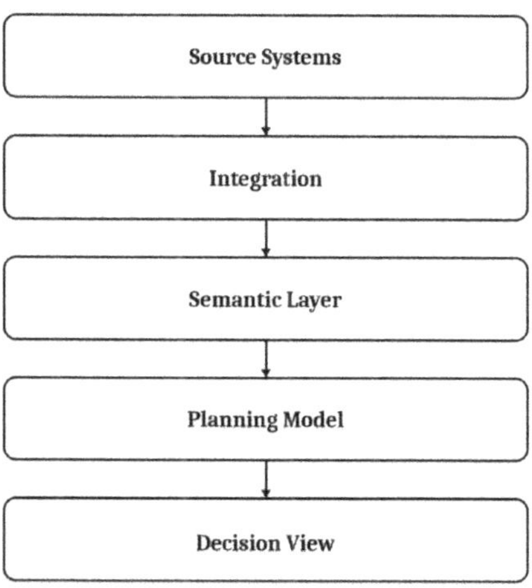

Figure 2 — Planning Stack

At a minimum, your stack has five layers. Source systems (ERP, CRM, HRIS, procurement, billing) hold the facts of activity. The integration layer moves those facts into the planning environment on a predictable cadence. The semantic layer defines meaning: what "revenue", "gross margin", "headcount", and "pipeline" mean, and how they are calculated. The planning model layer converts meaning into foresight through drivers, scenarios, and assumptions. The experience layer (dashboards and reports) delivers outputs leaders consume.

Most FP&A transitions fail because organisations modernise the experience layer while leaving meaning unresolved. They build beautiful dashboards on top of unstable definitions. Leaders then argue with the language of the numbers and abandon the tool.

This is why CFOs insist on a glossary and definition register early. It does not need to be perfect. It needs to be governed. Every critical metric should have a definition, an owner, and a change protocol. When a definition changes, the organisation should know what changed and from which date it applies.

Treat the semantic layer as your "metric engine". If you allow multiple calculation rules (Power BI formula here, Excel tweak there, analyst adjustment elsewhere), you create competing realities. The goal is one rule set that feeds both planning and reporting, so the business experiences continuity across dashboards, forecasts, and management packs.

A useful practice is to link each key dashboard view to a decision brief: the question it answers, the threshold for action, and the owner who acts when the threshold is breached. This turns reporting into operational motion and prevents metrics becoming wallpaper (Davenport and Harris, 2007).

Assign data stewardship explicitly. Someone must own the customer hierarchy, the product taxonomy, the cost centre structure, and the planning calendar. When master data ownership is vague, the system becomes "correct" in Finance and "wrong" everywhere else, which is the fastest way to lose adoption.

Cadence Design: Budget, Forecast, and Strategic Plan as One System

A FP&A system is not only a tool for the annual budget. It is the backbone for three connected horizons: the annual budget as the commitment, the rolling forecast as the navigation, and the multi-year plan as the direction.

Your platform transition is the moment to unify these horizons. Use the same drivers, the same definitions, and the same dimensional views (segment, region, product). Then set cadence rules so the business knows when the organisation is in "commitment mode" versus "navigation mode".

A practical cadence looks like this. The annual budget sets the baseline and becomes the reference plan in the system. The rolling forecast updates on a defined rhythm (monthly for most organisations; more frequently in high volatility) and is refreshed early if agreed triggers breach. Triggers are simple: forecast accuracy drift, material churn change, margin compression, or a cash runway threshold. The multi-year plan is reviewed quarterly as a direction check, not as a monthly re-forecast. When cadence is explicit, departments stop lobbying for exceptions and start treating forecasting as normal leadership behaviour.

The Stakeholder Contract: What Finance Promises, What the Business Commits

Adoption becomes durable when you set an explicit contract between Finance and the business. Without a contract, the organisation treats the platform as optional, and optional systems never survive crisis.

Finance commits to clear refresh times, stable definitions, rapid support during cycles, and transparent reconciliation when differences appear. The business commits to using the platform as the place where forecasts live, to submitting inputs on time, and to owning the drivers within their decision rights. Executives commit to using the system in meetings, because what leadership uses becomes organisational truth.

The First 100 Days After Go-Live

Go-live is the start of behavioural consolidation. The first one hundred days determine whether the organisation builds new habits or returns to old ones.

Days 1–30: protect trust. Run weekly clinics, reconcile openly, and publish a visible issues log with resolution status. Reinforce the one forecast doctrine: inputs belong in the platform, not in email attachments.

Days 31–60: build competence. Shift training from "how to click" to "how to interpret". Use real examples from live cycles and teach leaders to ask driver questions: what moved, why it moved, and what we can influence.

Days 61–100: lock in routines. Move executive meetings fully into the platform view, retire at least one legacy template permanently, and run a scenario drill to prove the organisation can use the system under pressure.

Across all one hundred days, the CFO models visible discipline: referencing drivers, using the platform in communications, and rewarding teams who adopt the new language. When leaders see the system used calmly under scrutiny, they stop needing the spreadsheet safety blanket.

Decommission Doctrine: The System Becomes Real When Excel Stops Being the Backup

The clearest indicator of successful FP&A transformation is behavioural: the organisation stops treating Excel as the "real forecast" and starts treating the platform as the shared reality.

This does not mean banning spreadsheets. It means ending the shadow process where spreadsheets hold the truth and the system holds the presentation.

Execute a decommission plan. Identify legacy templates and shadow models. Replace each artefact with a platform-native equivalent, even if imperfect. Set a date when forecasts will no longer be accepted outside the platform. Protect the business with clinics and rapid response support.

The CFO must model this discipline. If the CFO asks for Excel extracts "for comfort", the organisation will interpret that as proof the system is not reliable. In system transitions, leadership behaviour is policy.

Rollout Risk Register

Every FP&A transition carries predictable risks. CFOs name them early, build controls, and define early warning indicators before trust is damaged.

Risk 1: data quality contamination. If master data is inconsistent, outputs will not reconcile. Control: cleansing sprint, lineage documentation, and parallel reporting. Early warning: rising reconciliation hours and repeated manual adjustments.

Risk 2: definition drift. If revenue, margin, and cost classifications change without governance, leaders will argue instead of act. Control: KPI register, change control, and a single owner per definition. Early warning: repeated "what does this include" questions in meetings.

Risk 3: adoption theatre. People attend training but keep real work in spreadsheets. Control: meeting doctrine, one forecast doctrine, and measured adoption. Early warning: flat active usage and continued email attachments during forecast cycles.

Risk 4: integration fragility. If refresh timing is unreliable, trust collapses quickly. Control: stabilise critical pipelines first, publish refresh commitments, and monitor failures visibly. Early warning: leaders quoting "yesterday's numbers" as evidence the system is late.

Risk 5: model complexity creep. Custom demands expand until the model becomes unmaintainable. Control: driver discipline, minimal viable model, and quarterly model governance reviews. Early warning: model changes taking longer than forecast cycles.

Risk 6: change fatigue and resentment. The system becomes associated with pressure rather than clarity. Control: phased rollout, visible wins, and narrative discipline. Early warning: silence in training sessions and low question volume combined with low adoption.

Risk 7: vendor dependency. The organisation cannot operate the platform without permanent consultants. Control: internal capability builds, documentation, and clear ownership from day one. Early warning: every change request routed to external support.

Boards do not need an exhaustive risk list. They need confidence that you see the real risks and have controls that protect integrity.

Final Thought

An FP&A system isn't a finance tool. It is a decision platform, one that either accelerates clarity or multiplies confusion.

Your role isn't just to select a platform. It is to lead the integration of financial intelligence into how the organisation sees itself. To create one shared reality, one disciplined cadence, and one language for performance that leaders can trust.

Because every great decision needs structure. And every great structure begins with you.

Chapter 5 – Leading Through Change

Tools and prompts for transition readiness, adoption rhythm, and communication are consolidated in Appendix C – FP&A System Transition Playbook.

Building Confidence in the Midst of Uncertainty

The system is ready.

The budget is aligned.

The new cost centre structure is mapped.

Yet something is still missing: the human element.

No transformation succeeds on logic alone. It succeeds when people believe the change is real, feel supported through the discomfort of transition, and understand what is expected of them without having to guess. This is where many CFOs, despite strategic and operational excellence, lose momentum.

Because building the plan is one thing.
Leading people through the plan is something else entirely.

Financial transformation carries a unique tension. Finance is expected to be precise, controlled, measured. Change is uneven, emotional, and sometimes irrational. When you bring the two together, people do not only react to tools or process. They react to what the change implies about competence, scrutiny, safety, and status.

If the organisation senses that Finance is implementing rather than leading, adoption becomes compliance. If it senses that Finance is present, human, and clear, adoption becomes commitment.

Your job is not simply to manage change.
It is to lead it visibly, calmly, and with executive confidence.

Change Is Not the Problem. Confusion Is.

Contrary to popular belief, most employees do not resist change itself. They resist uncertainty that feels unmanaged. They resist being expected to perform in a new environment without clarity, training, or support. They resist when the "why" feels vague, the timeline feels rushed, and leadership behaviours stay unchanged while everyone else is asked to adapt.

In finance transformations, confusion shows up in predictable ways:

It shows up when people do not know which numbers to trust; people do not know what "good" looks like in the new process; people do not know whether mistakes will be punished or treated as learning; people do not know which process is temporary and which is now the standard; and people do not know who to ask, so they stop asking.

When people feel uncertain, they protect themselves. They revert to old habits, build shadow spreadsheets, delay decisions, and quietly wait for the change to pass. This is not laziness. It is self-preservation.

That is why the CFO must be a stabiliser. In transformation, your presence becomes a signal: this is coherent, this is supported, this is worth learning, and you will not be abandoned inside ambiguity.

Executive Case Insight: The Transformation That Was Technically Perfect and Culturally Dead

Many organisations experience the same pattern. The programme plan is clean. The vendor is satisfied. Data migration is complete. Training sessions are delivered. The dashboards look excellent.

Three months after launch, little has truly changed.

Leaders still request reports by email. Budget owners still track spend in their own spreadsheets. Variance discussions still revolve around blame instead of insight. The tool exists, but it is not used as the enterprise's decision surface.

The reasons are rarely technical. They are behavioural.

People were not included early enough, so they did not feel ownership. The purpose was framed as "Finance upgrading systems" rather than "the organisation gaining decision clarity". Training was delivered as instruction rather than confidence-building. Leaders were not seen using the new views in the rooms where decisions are made, so everyone assumed it was optional. Questions were met with impatience, so people stopped asking. Resistance was dismissed, so it moved underground.

The transformation was technically correct, but culturally it did not land.

This is the principle the Strategic CFO must hold: finance transformation is not primarily a system change. It is a trust change. Trust is built through how people experience leadership under uncertainty.

The CFO's Change Mandate: Stabilise, Translate, and Reinforce

There are three roles the CFO must play during change.

First, stabiliser. You reduce noise and create predictability. You make it safe to learn by making the environment coherent.

Second, translator. You convert finance logic into operational meaning. You explain trade-offs in language leaders can use.

Third, reinforcer. You make the new behaviours visible, rewarded, and normal. You close loops. You repeat the message until it becomes a shared habit.

When these three roles are performed consistently, adoption stops being a change programme and becomes a new operating standard.

The Change Readiness Scan: What You Must Know Before You Push

Before you intensify communication or accelerate rollout, take ten minutes to diagnose readiness. Not through a survey alone, but through executive observation.

Readiness is shaped by five conditions:

Change load: how many other programmes are currently running, and whether the organisation is already fatigued; trust level: whether people believe leadership tells the truth when pressure rises; capability baseline: whether managers can interpret financial information without relying on Finance to translate every line; data hygiene: whether the underlying inputs are stable enough to support a single view without constant manual correction; and consequence clarity: whether people know how performance will be assessed during the transition.

If any of these conditions are weak, the answer is not to abandon change. The answer is to adjust sequencing, tighten support, and strengthen narrative. A CFO who drives change without reading readiness does not create speed. They create backlash.

There is a subtle CFO skill here: setting the organisation's expectations about what "good" looks like during transition. In the early phase, good is not perfection. Good is participation, early escalation, and visible improvement. When that is stated clearly, people stop hiding and start learning.

Step 1: Establish a Clear Change Narrative

Every programme needs a simple story. Not a technical description. A story that people can repeat without improvising.

The narrative must answer four questions:

Leaders typically ask the same questions: "What is changing?"; "Why does it matter now?"; "What does success look like in daily work?"; and "What happens next, and how will we be supported?"

A weak narrative sounds like a system upgrade.
A strong narrative sounds like an executive capability shift.

For example:

"We are building a clearer planning and reporting system so every team can see their numbers, own their budgets, and act faster, with one shared version of reality and clear support."

Keep the language stable. If leaders hear three different reasons for the change in three different meetings, they will assume the change itself is unstable.

Tie the narrative to enterprise purpose. If volatility is high, position the new operating rhythm as resilience. If scale is rising, position the new structures as the only way to preserve accountability without drowning in complexity. If profitability is under pressure, position the new reporting and decision rhythms as the discipline that protects investment where it matters.

Then repeat the narrative with consistency. Repetition is not redundancy. Repetition is trust-building. By the time you are tired of hearing it, the organisation is just beginning to believe it.

Step 2: Build a Coalition of Influencers

Change does not travel through reporting lines. It travels through trust networks.

Successful CFOs build a coalition, not a committee. They identify the people others listen to when uncertain, and they involve them early enough that they can shape the rollout rather than merely receive it.

Build your coalition across budget owners and high-influence managers; practical operators who know how work gets done; analysts and super-users who will become informal teachers; HR and People partners who can see the human temperature; and procurement and IT leaders who control connected workflows (Kotter, 1996).

Give coalition members roles, not just invitations. Let them test the new process. Ask them where language is unclear, where steps feel heavy, and where confidence is likely to drop. Use them to translate finance constructs into operational relevance.

Recognise their contribution openly. If champions feel invisible, they burn out. If champions feel respected, they become carriers of credibility.

One discipline matters here: the coalition is not a marketing function. It is an early-warning system. You are buying realism. You are turning feedback into resilience before launch.

Step 3: Create Tools for Confidence, Not Just Compliance

People do not adopt what they understand intellectually. They adopt what they can do reliably under pressure (Kotter, 1996).

Adoption requires confidence. Confidence comes from small wins, visible support, and practical scaffolding.

Confidence-building tools are precise. They answer the questions people are often afraid to ask:

Leaders typically ask the same questions: "What do I do differently now?"; "How do I know I am doing it correctly?"; "What happens if I make a mistake?"; "Who helps me when I get stuck?"; and "What is the fastest way to get this done without reverting to the old method?"

Build a support architecture with at least five elements.

1) Role-based walkthroughs

Budget owners need different training than analysts. Managers need interpretation, not buttons. Executives need decision views, not navigation.

2) One-page guides and "first ten minutes" checklists

Short, plain-language guides reduce anxiety. They help people act without waiting.

3) Office hours

A predictable slot each week where people can ask questions without judgement. The goal is not perfection. The goal is willingness to try.

4) A visible help route

One email address or channel, with agreed response time and escalation. If people do not know where to go, they go back to Excel.

5) Demonstrations in real leadership rooms

The moment leaders see the new dashboard used in a performance review; it becomes real. If it is not used at the top, it will not be used at the edges.

Finance does not need everyone to be experts. Finance needs people to feel competent enough to participate. Competence produces ownership. Ownership produces better forecasts, fewer surprises, and faster decisions.

Step 4: Build the Change Cadence

Most transformations fail not because the plan is wrong, but because the organisation loses orientation. People do not know what is happening, when it will change again, or where they should direct their energy.

The antidote is cadence.

The operating rhythm is the schedule of truth-telling, decision-making, and support. It creates psychological stability without removing accountability. It turns change into a sequence people can live through.

A strong change cadence has three layers.

Layer 1: Executive rhythm This is where strategic decisions are made, trade-offs are confirmed, and blockers are removed. In practice, this often looks like a fortnightly Steering Group, chaired by the CFO, focused on decisions and escalations; a monthly executive review that uses the new dashboards as the default decision surface; and a board update rhythm that focuses on risk, liquidity, delivery milestones, and adoption integrity.

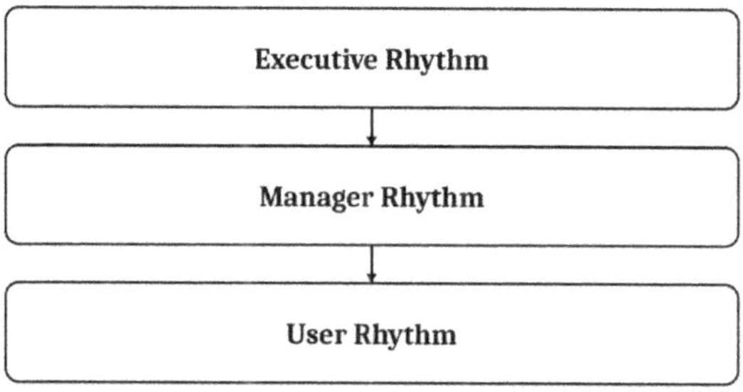

Figure 3 — Three-layer adoption rhythm

Layer 2: Manager rhythm This is where adoption becomes behaviour. In practice, this often looks like weekly team-level check-ins: what is working, what is unclear, what support is needed; a consistent monthly variance and forecast rhythm, using the new logic and definitions; and a short escalation route for blockers that managers cannot resolve alone.

Layer 3: User rhythm This is where confidence is built. In practice, this often looks like weekly office hours in the first twelve weeks; a champions sync that captures friction points and improvement requests; and micro-learning refreshes at week four, week eight, and week twelve, based on what users are struggling with.

The CFO's task is to make the rhythm predictable, brief, and visible. People should never have to wonder when they will hear the next update, or whether their questions will disappear into a project inbox.

Cadence also requires a decision log. Every programme creates version drift when decisions are made in different rooms and remembered differently. A decision log is a simple record of what we decided, why we decided it, and what changes for users. When this exists, political debate falls and operational speed rises.

A useful rule: if something changes in the process, communicate it in three places, the executive forum, the manager channel, and the user-facing guide. Consistency is not corporate formality. It is adoption protection.

Change Cadence as Governance: How to Prevent Drift and Version Chaos

This rhythm is not only communication. It is governance.

Every transformation creates version risk. Different teams interpret the change differently. People take shortcuts. Local managers create "temporary" workarounds that become permanent. Definitions drift. Trust erodes quietly.

To prevent this, your change cadence must include a change-control discipline: the rules that protect integrity while still allowing improvement.

Protect four things.

1) Definitions

If a KPI, driver, or forecast assumption changes, it must be documented, communicated, and time stamped. If definitions drift, accountability collapses.

2) Templates and inputs

If users are allowed to submit in multiple formats, you will spend your time reconciling. Standardise inputs early, then improve them rather than multiplying them.

3) Exceptions

Exceptions are sometimes necessary, but they must be treated as exceptions. If exceptions become routine, the organisation will build a shadow operating system.

4) Decision pathways

If people do not know who decides when friction appears, escalation becomes political. Publish the escalation route, keep it tight, and respond quickly.

This is not bureaucracy. It is integrity design. When the rules are clear, the organisation moves faster, because it spends less time debating what is true.

The 90-Day Adoption Arc: Orientation, Stabilisation, Optimisation

A disciplined CFO treats adoption as an arc, not a moment.

Days 1–30: Orientation

This is where people form beliefs. They decide whether the new system is real, whether leadership will stay present, and whether asking questions is safe.

Your focus is orientation, not performance perfection. In practice, this often looks like keep office hours weekly and respond quickly to common friction; publish short clarifications fast, and update guides when the reality changes; run executive reviews using the new dashboards, even if imperfect, so the organisation sees commitment; and maintain reconciliation views where necessary, but time-box them.

Days 31–60: Stabilisation

This is where habits either form or fail.

Your focus is stabilisation. In practice, this often looks like reduce friction points surfaced in the first month; tighten definitions and remove duplicate templates; move from "how to use" questions to "how to interpret" coaching; and begin tracking adoption metrics and addressing gaps through support, not shame.

Days 61–90: Optimisation
This is where the change becomes performance.

Your focus is optimisation. In practice, this often looks like codify the most effective practices into the permanent operating cadence; decommission legacy reports and shadow templates; strengthen governance triggers and escalation pathways; and introduce capability upgrades, such as driver-based forecasting refinements, scenario refresh routines, and sharper dashboards.

After ninety days, the work is no longer "change". It is the organisation's new standard. The transition period ends when the new way becomes the default without discussion.

The CFO's Non-Negotiables During Change

There are moments when your leadership must be firm. Not harsh, but firm. Transformation fails when leadership signals that adherence is optional.

Non-negotiables that protect adoption:

One shared forecast. One set of assumptions. No private alternative numbers used for executive decisions. One decision surface: dashboards and reporting views used in leadership forums must be the same ones used by budget owners. One route for exceptions: if a team cannot comply, they escalate early, and the exception is documented with a path back to standard. One vocabulary: if Finance uses one term and Operations uses another, you will spend your time resolving language, not performance.

These non-negotiables must be stated calmly, early, and consistently. People do not follow what is implied. They follow what is explicit.

When Senior Leaders Undermine the Change

A common, uncomfortable truth is that adoption often fails because senior leaders quietly bypass the new process.

An executive asks for the old report "just for this meeting".

A director sends a spreadsheet because it is faster.

A senior leader requests a bespoke metric view that breaks the standard definitions.

If you allow this, the organisation learns the following lesson: the new system is for everyone else, not for leadership. Adoption will die quietly.

Handle senior bypassing with calm clarity.

Script:

"I can get you that view, but I will not create a parallel truth. Let's solve this inside the new system so everyone works from the same reality. If something is missing, we add it properly with definitions, rather than creating an off-system report."

You are not refusing support. You are protecting integrity.

The Change Cadence in Practice: What to Do, and When

A structured change rhythm is not constant messaging. It is a predictable sequence of forums that keep the organisation oriented.

Pre-launch, four to six weeks before go-live In practice, this often looks like announce the narrative and the timeline; identify champions and run preview sessions; publish the "what changes for you" guide by role; run a live demo for leadership and budget owners, using real examples; and open the help route and confirm response times.

Weeks 1–2: go-live and initial adoption In practice, this often looks like daily or every-other-day leadership check-ins for the core decision group, focused on blockers and integrity risks; two office-hour slots per week, then reduce as confidence rises; and a short end-of-week update: what changed, what stabilised, what we fixed, what happens next.

Weeks 3–4: stabilise behaviours In practice, this often looks like move office hours to weekly; begin simple adoption reporting: participation, submission timeliness, major friction categories; and run the first retrospective with champions and managers, then publish the improvements.

Weeks 5–8: tighten and embed In practice, this often looks like shift from support-heavy to coaching-heavy; lock definitions and reduce reconciliation views; begin decommissioning legacy templates in phases; and hold a leadership calibration session: what is the new decision rhythm, and what is now the standard.

Weeks 9–12: codify and normalise In practice, this often looks like convert lessons into permanent guidance; formalise the ongoing cadence for forecast refresh and variance action; and close out the change programme with an explicit "now standard" communication: what is final, what is evolving, and how improvements will be governed.

This rhythm is not a rigid playbook. It is a structure you adjust to your context. The principle is what matters: predictability reduces anxiety, and reduced anxiety increases adoption speed.

Step 5: Communicate Progress, Not Just Tasks

Milestones matter, but people do not attach psychologically to milestone lists. They attach to progress they can feel.

Change communication should be short, regular, and impact focused.

A strong weekly update answers: Leaders typically ask the same questions: "What changed since last week?"; "What is stable?"; "What happens next?"; "What support is available?"; and "What did we learn and adjust?"

Speak in the language of outcomes. In practice, this often looks like "Forecast refresh is now two days, not seven."; "Budget owners can see spend drivers without waiting for Finance."; "We reduced manual reclassifications by half."; and "Variance conversations are shifting from explanation to action.".

Progress communication should also include gratitude. Transformation is labour. People are adjusting while still doing their day jobs. Recognition is not sentiment. It is a trust strategy and a retention strategy.

Silence after launch is dangerous. When communication disappears, people assume the change has stopped mattering. When communication continues with consistency, people assume the change is real.

Step 6: Channel Friction Without Letting It Derail You

Resistance is not always opposition. Often it is data. It is a signal that something is unclear, misaligned, or too heavy.

When leaders dismiss resistance, they do not eliminate it. They drive it underground, where it becomes silent sabotage: shadow reporting, partial adoption, and disengagement.

An CFO channels friction into improvement without surrendering authority.

Do three things consistently.

First, listen for the category of resistance. Is this a capability gap, a workload reality, a trust concern, or a status concern?

Second, name what is flexible and what is fixed. Uncertainty about flexibility is one of the fastest routes to anxiety. If leaders do not know what can be adjusted, they assume either everything is negotiable or nothing is negotiable. Both create dysfunction.

Third, respond with calm structure. If you become defensive, you teach the organisation that the change cannot withstand scrutiny. If you remain steady, you teach the organisation that concerns can be surfaced early without punishment.

This is where language becomes one of your most powerful tools.

Resistance Handling Scripts: Language That Keeps Authority and Trust

The goal of these scripts is not to "win" arguments. The goal is to keep the room stable, protect legitimacy, and move the organisation toward usable clarity.

1) "This is adding more work."
Response:

"I agree it feels heavier at the start. The short-term cost is learning. The long-term payoff is fewer reconciliations, fewer surprises, and faster decisions. Tell me which step is creating the extra work and we will simplify it, but we are not going back to fragmented versions."

2) "The numbers don't match what we're used to."
Response:

"Let's separate two issues. If the number is wrong, we fix it. If the number is unfamiliar because the structure changed, we explain it. We will run a reconciliation view for this cycle so you can trace old to new, and then we will lock definitions, so the organisation has one shared truth."

3) "Finance doesn't understand our reality."
Response:

"Your reality is exactly why we are doing this. The current model forces you to defend costs you cannot influence. This redesign is about matching ownership to levers. Help us identify where influence is misaligned, and we will correct the structure. The goal is legitimacy, not control."

4) "This will be used to blame us."
Response:

"This is not a blame tool. It is a decision tool. If a metric is used as punishment, people will hide, and the organisation will get weaker. We will treat variance as a signal for action, and accountability will be paired with support and clear levers."

5) "We are too busy for training."
Response:

"I respect the load. That is why training will be short and role based. But skipping training creates more time loss later through rework and confusion. Choose a slot this week. Ten focused minutes now saves hours of friction later."

6) "We can't hit these targets."
Response:

"Let's treat that as information, not failure. If the target is unrealistic, we need to surface the trade-off now, not in month-end surprise. Bring two options: what you can deliver with current resources, and what changes if we adjust investment or scope. Then leadership decides consciously."

7) "Excel is faster."
Response:

"Excel is fast for one person, and slow for the enterprise. It creates multiple truths and forces reconciliation. We will still use spreadsheets for analysis where it adds value, but the shared forecast and performance view will live in one system, so decisions are anchored to one reality."

8) "This will slow approvals."
Response:

"Approvals slow down when decision rights are unclear. We will publish the decision path and escalation route, and we will keep sign-offs tight. If an approval takes more than forty-eight hours, we will treat that as a governance failure to fix, not as a new normal."

These scripts work because they do three things at once. They acknowledge emotion without surrendering direction. They offer a practical next step. They reinforce the non-negotiable principle: one shared way of working.

More Resistance Scripts: The Conversations That Protect Trust

Not all resistance is expressed politely. Some comes as sarcasm, withdrawal, or quiet non-compliance. The CFO's advantage is disciplined calm.

Use language that names the issue without escalating it.

9) "This keeps changing. We can't keep up."
Response:

"You're right. Change without stability becomes noise. That's why we are locking definitions on a monthly cycle and only changing what is essential. If you see drift, escalate it, and we will protect stability. You should not have to guess what is true."

10) "This feels like Finance is taking control."
Response:

"Control is not the goal. Clarity is. The aim is for you to have better visibility and levers, not less autonomy. If any step reduces your ability to run your area, we will redesign it, but we will not compromise the shared truth that enables the enterprise to move together."

11) "We're being asked to do more with less."
Response:

"I won't pretend that isn't hard. The question is how we protect capability while tightening cost. We will separate essential work from legacy work, and we will remove low-value reporting, so your effort goes into decisions, not administration. Bring me the reporting that feels like theatre, and we will cut it."

12) "I don't want my team exposed by this level of transparency."
Response:

"Transparency is not exposure. It is early signal. The earlier we see drift, the earlier we can support. We will focus on trends and actions, not humiliation. If a forum becomes punitive, tell me immediately. We protect dignity, because dignity protects truth-telling."

13) "The tool is still buggy, so we can't rely on it."
Response:

"If there is a defect, we log it, prioritise it, and time-box the workaround. But we do not abandon the system because it is imperfect. We stabilise it by using it, fixing it, and improving it. If we step away, the defects will never be resolved, and the old chaos will return."

14) "Why are we doing this now?"
Response:

"Because our current way of working is costing us speed, trust, and decision quality. Waiting does not make the problem smaller. It makes it more expensive. This programme is how we protect performance in the year ahead, and it is how we give leaders clearer levers under pressure."

These scripts matter because they remove the two extremes that damage change: defensiveness and softness. You remain firm on principles and generous on support.

The Manager Cascade Pack: How You Help Leaders Speak for the Change

Many transformations fail at the middle layer. Executives understand the programme, Finance understands the mechanics, but managers are left improvising how to explain it to their teams. Improvisation produces mixed messages. Mixed messages produce anxiety. Anxiety produces non-compliance.

Provide managers with a cascade pack that is short, usable, and consistent.

Include three elements.

1) A two-minute opener

"This change is about giving us one clear view of our numbers and making decisions faster. The early weeks will feel unfamiliar, and that is normal. Our job is to learn the new rhythm, surface blockers early, and keep the work moving."

2) A question-and-answer set Answer the questions managers know will come: Leaders typically ask the same questions: "What changes for our team this month?"; "What does good look like while we learn?"; "What happens if we get it wrong?"; "Where do we get help?"; and "What is not changing?"

3) Boundary language that protects integrity Managers need permission to be firm without being harsh.

"We are not keeping private numbers. We will use the shared dashboard, and if something looks wrong, we escalate it and fix it."
"We will not shame mistakes. We will correct them and improve the process."
"If you are stuck, raise it early. Silence makes problems expensive."

When managers have language, they stop avoiding conversations. When they stop avoiding conversations, adoption accelerates.

Step 7: Sustain the Change Beyond Launch

Go-live is not the finish line. It is the beginning of habit formation.

The months after launch are where old patterns attempt to return. Leaders are busy. Teams revert to what is comfortable. Shadow processes reappear "just in case". If you want durability, you must design reinforcement.

Reinforcement is not policing. It is continued leadership presence.

Three moves protect long-term adoption.

First, keep executive rooms honest. If executive reviews stop using the new dashboards, the organisation will interpret that as permission to ignore them. Use the new system as your default language.

Second, measure adoption as behaviour, not sentiment. Track: who is submitting forecasts on time; how many manual adjustments remain; how often dashboards are accessed; how many definitions are being questioned; how long it takes to close the variance loop from insight to action. These are operational signals. They tell you where to support, simplify, or reinforce.

Third, build the post-launch reset. At day thirty, day sixty, and day ninety, hold short retrospectives. Ask: what is working, what is heavy, what is unclear, what is being bypassed, and what must be codified. Then publish the improvements. When users see that the process evolves based on reality, trust rises.

A useful doctrine is that the new way must become easier than the old way. That is not achieved by forcing people. It is achieved by reducing friction until old habits feel inefficient rather than safe.

The Emotional Curve of Adoption: What You Should Expect

Even in high-performing cultures, adoption follows a predictable emotional curve.

At first, there is denial or minimisation: "We will see if these lasts."
Then frustration: "This is harder than the old way."
Then experimentation: "I think I can make this work."
Then commitment: "This is now the standard."

A CFO who expects this curve leads with patience and discipline. You do not interpret early frustration as failure. You interpret it as normal friction that must be reduced through support, simplification, and consistent leadership.

The organisation does not need you to be endlessly positive. It needs you to be steady. Steadiness is what turns uncertainty into confidence.

Common Pitfalls

Even strong programmes derail in familiar ways.

Assuming logic is enough. Just because the change is rational does not mean people will adopt it. People adopt what they can live with, emotionally and practically.

Delegating presence. The CFO can delegate project management, but not leadership. In transformation, your presence is part of the control environment.

Fixating on tools. Tools matter, but adoption is driven by confidence, clarity, and repeated use in real decision rooms.

Silencing resistance. Disagreement is data. If feedback is treated as disloyalty, information disappears and sabotage grows.

Declaring success too early. Go-live is not success. Success is different behaviour six months later, with fewer surprises and stronger decision speed.

Final Thought

You are not just upgrading a system.
You are guiding people through discomfort, doubt, and growth.

The spreadsheets may run smoother. The budgets may align. The cost centres may finally make sense. But it is how people experience leadership during uncertainty that determines whether your transformation lasts or gets undone in silence.

Leadership in change is not force. It is clarity. It is presence. It is patience paired with resolve. It is the ability to hold the organisation steady while it learns a new way of working.

Lead the change.
With clarity.
With presence.
With heart.

Chapter 6: Budgeting Meets Culture

Governance and accountability templates that support cost-culture change are consolidated in Appendix D – Governance & Dashboard Templates.

Cost Leadership Without Losing the Human Core

There is a common misconception in business: that budgeting is a numbers process and culture is a people process, and the two rarely meet. Budgeting is one of the most culture-defining acts leadership performs. It is where values stop being adjectives and become allocations, where ambition becomes capacity, and where "what matters" is translated into what is funded, protected, delayed, or refused.

Nothing reveals your real culture like how you budget. The way you allocate money, cut costs, approve headcount, and postpone investment speaks louder than any mission statement. Culture is not primarily what you declare. Culture is what you repeatedly reward, tolerate, protect, and sacrifice. Budgeting is the moment those choices become visible, and therefore believable.

The Strategic CFO understands that budgeting is not neutral. It is cultural expression in numeric form. It is also leadership psychology in operational form. If people experience budgeting as punishment, the organisation learns fear: hoarding, bargaining, hiding risk, manipulating forecasts, and building silos that protect reputations rather than outcomes. If people experience budgeting as an enabling rhythm, the organisation learns ownership: early escalation, honest trade-offs, transparent assumptions, and shared responsibility for performance.

Cost leadership becomes dangerous only when it is divorced from humanity. Discipline does not require coldness. Discipline requires clarity, and clarity can be delivered with dignity. This chapter builds the bridge between performance and people, so you can lead cost and capital decisions without damaging the culture that makes execution possible.

Why Budgeting Is a Cultural Force

Budgets do not just control spend; they shape belief. They tell teams what is safe to prioritise, what is risky to propose, what is rewarded, and what will be ignored. When a business repeatedly funds capability building, experimentation, and leadership development, it creates an organisation that learns. When a business repeatedly funds only short-term output, it creates an organisation that performs under pressure but burns out, hides mistakes, and struggles to evolve (Senge, 1990).

The budget also sets the emotional tone of accountability. If variance is treated as moral failure, managers learn to defend and distort. If variance is treated as information, managers learn to explain, adjust, and improve. The difference is not the spreadsheet. The difference is the posture of leadership, and the CFO is often the visible carrier of that posture.

A budget cycle is an annual ritual of power. It answers questions people rarely ask directly: Who is trusted? Who is protected? What is negotiable? What is sacred? What happens when reality deviates from the plan? The answers become culture, and the culture becomes your future performance.

What Budgeting Tells People (Even When You Don't Say It)

Employees do not need a memo to understand priorities. They read them in patterns. When learning and development is cut first, people learn that growth is conditional. When wellbeing support is always "postponed until next quarter," people learn that strain is normalised. When headcount approvals depend on who has the strongest executive sponsor, people learn that relationships matter more than rationale. When bonuses reward only output, people learn that the number outranks the manner in which the number was achieved.

These messages are rarely spoken directly, but they are felt. "We say we value people, but we fund performance." "We say we want innovation, but we punish uncertainty." "We say we value integrity, but we reward short-term wins."

This is why budgets create culture faster than speeches. They create a repetitive experience. People stop listening to declared values and start listening to funded values. And when funded values contradict declared values, trust quietly erodes.

Executive Case Insight: The Quiet Culture Collapse of "Efficiency"

In many organisations, cost reduction is launched under the banner of efficiency. The logic is sound: protect margin, reduce waste, align cost with reality. Yet the lived experience is often different. Budgets are cut without explanation. Hiring is frozen with no narrative. Teams are asked to deliver more with less, while leadership continues visible spend that feels disconnected from daily strain. Managers are held accountable for targets without being given levers. Finance is positioned as the enforcer, not the guide.

Within months, people do not just feel cost pressure; they feel betrayal. The organisation may hit short-term numbers, but it quietly pays a deeper price: retention declines, trust collapses, managers stop escalating risk early, and leaders begin to game the system rather than improve it. Performance becomes fragile. The CFO who understands culture can still lead cost transformation, but with an approach that protects legitimacy. Discipline without legitimacy creates resistance. Discipline with legitimacy creates ownership.

The Three Cost Cultures That Shape Behaviour

Most organisations, often without realising it, operate from one of three cost cultures. You can hear it in their language, see it in their approval patterns, and feel it in their decision latency. None of these cultures is "good" or "bad" in isolation; each can be appropriate in certain conditions. The risk comes when the culture is unconscious, inconsistent, or mismatched with the strategy you claim to pursue.

Figure 4 — Three Cost Cultures

1) Scarcity Culture: Control as Survival

In a scarcity cost culture, money is treated as a threat. The dominant leadership emotion is fear of being exposed, being overrun, or being judged. Approvals become defensive. Requests are assumed to be inflated. Each department is expected to fight for itself, and finance conversations become negotiations rather than planning.

Scarcity culture often emerges after crisis, in turnaround environments, or in organisations that have been punished for overspending. It can produce rapid savings and short-term liquidity protection, but it also creates predictable side effects. Managers stop asking for what they need. They delay decisions until forced. They reframe investment as "mandatory" because discretionary spend feels unsafe. Talent development becomes a luxury. Innovation becomes a slogan. Forecasts become political documents because the safest number is not the most accurate number; it is the number least likely to attract blame.

As CFO, you may need moments of scarcity discipline. The leadership requirement is to name it, time-box it, and prevent it from becoming Finance's permanent identity. Scarcity is an operating mode, not a personality. If you do not make that explicit, the organisation will internalise fear as a cultural norm, and long-term performance will erode.

2) Stewardship Culture: Discipline as Trust

In a stewardship culture, money is treated as a shared resource with a clear purpose. The dominant leadership emotion is responsibility. The organisation believes cost discipline and human dignity can co-exist, and that budget owners can be held accountable without being humiliated. Stewardship does not avoid hard decisions; it makes them with clarity and explanation.

Stewardship cultures have explicit principles. They define what will be protected and why. They teach managers how to plan. They make assumptions visible. They treat variance as learning and action, not shame. They also define the difference between waste and investment, and they recognise that cost reduction without capability protection is not discipline; it is organisational self-harm. For most enterprises, stewardship is the healthiest long-term cost culture because it builds trust, and trust reduces the cost of control. When people trust the process, they stop gaming it.

3) Investment Culture: Capital as a Growth Engine

In an investment culture, money is treated as fuel. The dominant leadership emotion is ambition. The organisation believes strategic bets, capability building, and long-term positioning are worth disciplined investment. This culture is common in growth phases, innovation-led businesses, and organisations with strong capital access.

Investment culture can generate speed and creativity, but it carries hidden risks. If "growth" becomes a blanket justification, discipline weakens. Teams begin to assume that funding will arrive because the narrative is exciting. Spending fragments into parallel initiatives that do not add up to a coherent strategy. Leaders reward storytelling over evidence, and the hard work of stopping non-performing initiatives is postponed until the costs are too visible to ignore.

The CFO does not reject investment culture; they professionalise it. They install guardrails that preserve ambition while protecting integrity: clear investment criteria, stage gates, leading indicators that are reviewed on cadence, and a willingness to stop what is not working without punishing the people who surfaced the truth. Investment culture without stop-discipline becomes drift; investment culture with stop-discipline becomes strategic motion.

How to Diagnose Your Cost Culture in One Week

The practical question is not "What cost culture do we believe we have?" It is "What cost culture are people experiencing?" The answer lives in patterns. How quickly do approvals happen? How often do teams escalate risk early? Do managers ask for help, or hide until month end? Do people believe Finance is fair and consistent, or unpredictable and political? Do leaders explain trade-offs, or announce cuts without narrative?

Spend a week listening. In budget reviews, note which phrases dominate: "We can't afford that," "Just make it work," "We'll see," or "Let's choose what we protect." In leadership meetings, observe whether numbers are used as weapons or as orientation. Culture is not a poster. It is a repeated experience. Your job is to choose, deliberately, which cost culture you will run, and to communicate that stance so people know what to expect.

Moving Between Cost Cultures Without Losing Credibility

Cost culture is not static. A mature enterprise can move between cultures as conditions change, but only if the shift is deliberate and narrated. The problem is not that organisations become tighter or looser; the problem is that they change mood without changing rules. When governance feels inconsistent, people stop trusting Finance. They then create their own rules in the shadows, and your budgeting discipline weakens.

When conditions tighten, the CFO may need to introduce scarcity discipline: a temporary freeze, faster approvals, stricter investment gating, and a sharper focus on liquidity. The key is to frame it as a protective regime with clear triggers. Say what has changed in the environment, say what you are protecting, and say what will reopen. A scarcity posture becomes culturally damaging when it is indefinite, unexplained, or applied unevenly.

When conditions stabilise, the CFO should actively shift the organisation back into stewardship. That means re-opening planning conversations, returning decision rights to budget owners, and reinstating learning signals rather than fear signals. If you do not deliberately return to stewardship, people will retain crisis behaviours: hoarding, defensive forecasting, and quiet disengagement. Those behaviours remain long after the crisis has passed and become the hidden reason performance feels harder than it should.

In growth phases, the CFO can support an investment culture without surrendering discipline by making investment professional. That includes explicit criteria, stage gates, and "stop rules." A stop rule is not cynicism; it is respect for capital and respect for truth. It tells teams: we will invest when indicators are strong, and we will stop when indicators fail, without blaming people for learning. This is how you preserve ambition and protect integrity at the same time.

The CFO as Culture Translator

Many executives treat culture as something felt and finance as something counted. The Strategic CFO translates between the two so that culture becomes operational, and finance becomes human. You translate culture into resource rules: what is protected, what is funded, what must be earned, and what must stop. You translate finance into language leaders can use without fear: what a variance means, what a forecast is signalling, and what decisions are now required.

Translation also requires a deliberate shift in how Finance speaks about cost. When cost is framed as punishment, leaders respond with defensiveness and hiding. When cost is framed as stewardship, leaders respond with ownership and trade-off thinking. The difference is often a few words. Compare "You overspent" with "Your run rate has moved; what changed and what do we decide?" Compare "This is not in budget" with "What would we stop to fund it?"

Compare "You missed target" with "Which driver moved and what are the options?"

If you want psychological safety without losing standards, separate people from numbers. Numbers are outputs; behaviours are inputs. The CFO can hold standards by asking for evidence, clarity, and action, while refusing humiliation, sarcasm, or public blame. In organisations, it is normal for leaders to say, "I don't know yet, but I will return with the analysis," because that honesty is rewarded, not punished (Edmondson, 2019).

Finally, remember that budgeting is a leadership classroom. Every review meeting teaches managers how to think. If you teach them that budget conversations are about defence, they will become defensive. If you teach them that budget conversations are about decision and learning, they will become better leaders. Over time, the organisation's budgeting maturity becomes the organisation's leadership maturity.

Consistency is the quiet currency of trust. If rules change, explain why. If exceptions are made, record them. If priorities shift, update the narrative, not just the spreadsheet. People do not resist discipline; they resist surprise.

Step 1: Define Cultural Alignment in Budgeting

Cultural alignment in budgeting means ensuring that spending, saving, and strategic priorities reflect how you want your people to feel, act, and believe. It is the deliberate practice of designing budgets, they support not only outcomes, but the behaviours and capabilities that sustain those outcomes.

Begin by naming the cultural priorities that truly matter in your context. Is the organisation trying to become more innovative? More accountable? More inclusive? More customer-centric? More operationally excellent? More resilient in uncertainty? Then ask the harder questions: where is there a gap between what we say and what we fund? Where are we asking people to behave one way while budgets reward another? Where does leadership language promise care while budget decisions signal indifference?

This gap is your opportunity. Aligning budgets with culture does not necessarily mean spending more. It means spending with meaning. It means protecting what creates long-term capability, not only what protects short-term optics. It means allocating in a way that makes your stated values believable.

Step 2: Audit the Budget for Cultural Impact

Run a culture-conscious review of your budget cycle. Not as a soft exercise, but as a strategic diagnostic. Budgets reinforce behaviour. If you want different behaviour, you must examine the signals your budget currently sends.

Look at patterns across people investment, incentives, inclusion and belonging, communication, and trust. Are learning and development budgets protected, or cut first? Are incentives tied only to numbers, or also to stewardship behaviours? Are inclusion initiatives resourced with legitimacy, or treated as symbolic? Are budget discussions open and collaborative, or guarded and top-down? Do managers feel ownership of their numbers, or fear and suspicion?

Do not rely only on what leaders say. Study what happens in the room. In healthy budgeting cultures, managers bring early signals and ask for help. In unhealthy budgeting cultures, managers bring polished narratives and hide risk until it is too late. The quality of information is itself a cultural indicator. When information becomes performative, you are paying a cultural tax in every forecast.

Budget Language and Emotional Safety

Budgeting is an emotional process disguised as a technical one. The spreadsheet is tangible, but the experience is psychological. For many managers, budgeting triggers fear of exposure: fear of being judged, fear of losing headcount, fear of being blamed for performance they cannot fully control. When fear drives the room, the budget becomes less accurate, not more.

The CFO can change this by building emotional safety through language and design. Emotional safety is not softness. It is clarity without threat. It is the ability to tell the truth early without being punished for naming reality.

Language creates safety or danger faster than policy. Consider the difference between: "We need you to cut ten per cent," and "We need to close a gap, and we will do it together by choosing what we protect and what we pause." The first triggers defence. The second triggers problem-solving.

Budget language makes constraints explicit without blaming people, honours ownership, normalises uncertainty, and frames trade-offs as leadership rather than punishment. It shifts the conversation from "defend your number" to "explain your plan." It also avoids humiliation. A leader who is publicly shamed for variance will teach everyone else to hide variance. In that environment, Finance may feel strict, but it will become blind.

A practical ritual that builds safety is the assumptions-first rule. Begin budget conversations with shared assumptions: demand, price, inflation, wage changes, capacity constraints. When assumptions are explicit, debates become rational. When assumptions are hidden, debates become personal.

Emotional safety also shows up in escalation. In culture, escalation is not a punishment ladder. It is a support ladder. People raise issues early because doing so is framed as professionalism. When CFOs treat early escalation as competence, the organisation becomes more honest and therefore more controllable.

Step 3: Integrate Culture into Budget Guidance

When issuing annual budget guidance, include cultural priorities as explicit design constraints, not inspirational language. If innovation is a strategic priority, guidance should protect experimentation and capability building even during cost pressure. If retention is a priority, guidance should protect manager development and onboarding quality. If customer experience is a priority, guidance should prevent short-term cuts that silently destroy service capacity.

Invite departments to submit qualitative context alongside numbers. Encourage a short narrative: what outcomes this budget supports, what risks exist, and what would break if the budget were cut. This is not storytelling for its own sake. It is operational intelligence. Treating budget owners as leaders, not petitioners, improves the quality of plans and increases accountability.

Values-Backed Budgeting: Funding What You Claim

Most organisations have a values gap. They say they value people, but development budgets are always first to go. They say they value innovation, but experimentation money is unprotected and approvals are slow. They say they value inclusion, but funding is symbolic and inconsistent. People do not become cynical because values exist; they become cynical because values are unfunded.

Values-backed budgeting closes the gap by aligning resource signals with stated priorities. It can be implemented without adding cost by changing what is protected, how decisions are made, and how trade-offs are explained.

A practical framework is to categorise spend into four intentions: protect, improve, invest, and stop. Protect spend sustains core delivery and risk integrity. Improve spend removes friction and releases time. Invest spend builds future capability and growth. Stop spend ends activity that no longer serves strategy. This approach moves the organisation away from blanket cuts and toward strategic choice.

As CFO, you strengthen values-backed budgeting with four disciplines: protecting a small set of capability lines that are non-negotiable because they sustain performance; requiring a values impact reflection for major cuts or freezes; aligning incentives so that how results are achieved matters; and narrating the budget as a story of priorities rather than a list of constraints.

When values are consistently funded, people stop treating culture as theatre. They begin to trust leadership intent, and trust improves planning quality. Better planning reduces unpleasant surprises. Fewer surprises reduce the need for reactive control. This is how culture becomes a financial advantage.

Dignity-Preserving Cost Leadership

Cost leadership is unavoidable. Even in growth phases, every organisation must make trade-offs. The question is not whether you will cut; it is whether you will cut in a way that preserves dignity, trust, and execution capability.

Dignity-preserving cost leadership follows a sequence. Start with waste, not people. Waste is anything that does not improve customer outcomes, risk posture, or capability. Redundant tools, duplicated processes, low-value spend that exists because "we always did it."

When you cut waste first, you signal competence, not brutality.

Then simplify before you reduce. Many costs are symptoms of complexity. Complexity creates meetings, workarounds, rework, and handoffs. Process simplification can release cost without cutting headcount, and it improves morale because people feel their time is respected.

Next, cut with narrative. Silence creates fear, and fear destroys productivity. If you must reduce budgets, explain the why, explain the method, and explain what is protected. People can live with hard decisions. They struggle with unexplained decisions.

Finally, distribute the burden fairly. If cuts concentrate on the frontline while leadership spend remains untouched, you create moral injury. Fairness is not only an ethical principle; it is a performance principle. People will not bring their best effort to a system they experience as unfair.

A CFO who leads cost decisions with dignity also protects managerial legitimacy. Managers need language and support to lead through constraint. When Finance equips managers with clear rules and credible narrative, the organisation maintains coherence under pressure.

The Dignity Playbook: How to Cut Without Cultural Damage

When cost actions become necessary, the CFO's job is to turn an emotional shock into a managed sequence. A practical dignity playbook is built on seven moves.

First, establish the non-negotiables. These are the capabilities you will protect because they keep the organisation safe, coherent, and able to deliver: critical customer pathways, regulatory and control integrity, key system reliability, and manager capacity where burnout risk is high. In cost action, what you protect defines who you are.

Second, separate structural costs from discretionary costs. If the business has a structural cost problem, a discretionary freeze will only delay pain. If the business has a discretionary sprawl problem, structural cuts may be unnecessary. Naming the type of cost problem prevents performative cutting.

Third, sequence levers from least damaging to most damaging. Renegotiate suppliers, simplify processes, consolidate tools, stop low-value initiatives, redesign working practices, then consider headcount levers only when other levers are insufficient. This is not compassioning theatre. It is operational intelligence: cutting the wrong muscle weakens recovery.

Fourth, create clarity on time horizon. Many cultural injuries occur because cost actions are framed as permanent when they are temporary or framed as temporary when they are permanent. If a freeze is for a defined period with defined review triggers, say so. If an initiative is being stopped, do not keep it alive through vague language. People adapt faster to truth than to ambiguity.

Fifth, equip leaders to communicate. The CFO should provide a simple narrative that managers can repeat without distortion: what changed, why it matters, what we are doing, what we are protecting, and what we need from teams. When managers lack narrative, they fill the gap with their own fear, and fear spreads.

Sixth, preserve dignity in execution. When roles must change, treat people as humans, not as entries on a spreadsheet. Be consistent, avoid surprise, and provide clarity on support. Even those who remain are watching what happened. The way you treat exits shapes the culture of those who stay.

Seventh, reset the operating rhythm after the cut. Cost actions without rhythm create lingering anxiety. Rhythm creates stability. A weekly review of liquidity, capacity, and priority focus tells people that leadership is present, not hiding. It also reduces the temptation to rebuild shadow budgets and workarounds.

Step 4: Use Finance to Model the Culture You Want

If Finance wants to lead cultural alignment, it must begin with its own posture. Culture does not change through policies alone; it changes through how leaders behave under pressure. The CFO's tone in budgeting season becomes a model that others copy.

Ask: do we collaborate with empathy and clarity? Are we approachable, or feared? Do we explain decisions, or only enforce them? Do we treat budget owners as partners, or as obstacles? A budget process can be structured without being harsh. It can be disciplined without humiliation. It can be demanding without being dehumanising.

Use monthly review meetings not only to track numbers, but to ask higher-quality questions: What changed? What does it mean? What support is needed? What do we do next? When you shift the tone from interrogation to decision, you strengthen both performance and culture.

Step 5: Communicate the Why Behind Budget Choices

Sometimes values-based budgeting means funding programmes without immediate ROI, protecting costs that drive engagement or creativity, or choosing long-term loyalty over short-term margin. These decisions are often misunderstood unless narrated well. This is where the CFO becomes more than a controller; the CFO becomes a storyteller of strategic intent.

Explain how a people investment supports retention and resilience, how capability protects delivery risk, how disciplined investment prevents future cost shocks, and how inclusion and belonging reduce attrition and improve performance. The organisation does not need marketing language. It needs a credible explanation of trade-offs. When Finance connects numbers to people, resistance turns into resonance.

The Budget as a Behavioural Contract

A budget is not simply an allocation. It is a behavioural contract between leadership and the organisation. Leadership says, "Here is what we expect." The organisation asks, "Will you support us to deliver it?"

If the budget demands more output but removes the resources needed to deliver, you create a breach of contract. The result is not only underperformance; it is distrust. Managers stop believing leadership is serious. They begin to protect themselves. They stop escalating reality early. Your financial control weakens.

CFOs treat budgets as commitments, not only targets. They insist on clarity about what is required, what can flex, and what will trigger re-planning. They also insist on explicit decision rights, so managers know when to act and when to escalate. When budgets become behavioural contracts, accountability becomes healthier, and the organisation becomes faster.

Three Budget Designs That Reinforce Culture

You do not change culture by issuing a memo. You change culture by redesigning the rhythm and structure through which people make decisions. Three design moves consistently reinforce a healthier budgeting culture.

First, build a shared assumptions pack. When each department budgets with different assumptions, budget debates become political. A shared assumptions pack creates fairness and coherence. It reduces emotional tension because teams are not punished for assumptions they could not control.

Second, create a protected reforecast cadence. If budgets are treated as fixed promises, managers learn to hide change until the last moment. A disciplined reforecast cadence tells managers: change will happen, and we will update reality together. This reduces fear and increases speed.

Third, install a decision-grade variance review. Instead of asking, "Why are you off plan?", ask, "What changed, what does it mean, and what do we do next?" This turns reviews into action, not blame. Culture improves because meetings become productive rather than performative.

Budgeting Through Volatility: Holding Humanity Under Pressure

The true test of culture-aligned budgeting is not when performance is strong. It is when pressure arrives. Under pressure, leaders tend to tighten control, cut quickly, and communicate less. That instinct is understandable, but it is often counterproductive.

In volatile conditions, you need a two-regime budgeting stance. In a benign regime, you operate with empowerment and learning. You encourage thoughtful investment and honest variance discussion. In a tight regime, you operate with increased discipline and faster cadence, but you preserve dignity through transparency and consistent rules. Tight regime does not mean fear regime; it means clarity regime.

This is where the CFO's emotional intelligence becomes a financial asset. If leadership escalates anxiety, the organisation becomes less accurate and more political. If leadership holds calm, the organisation becomes more honest and more adaptive. Calm is not an emotion. Calm is a leadership choice that protects performance.

Step 6: Make Culture Measurable Without Making It Mechanical

If budgeting shapes culture, then the CFO must be able to track cultural impact without reducing culture to slogans. The aim is not to measure feelings. The aim is to measure the operational signals that show whether the organisation is healthy under pressure.

Look for indicators such as forecast honesty, seen in how early teams surface downside; variance explanations, seen in whether managers describe drivers or excuses; leadership follow-through, seen in whether protected priorities stay protected; talent signal stability, seen in retention and internal mobility; and decision latency, seen in how quickly trade-offs are made.

These indicators are culture in action. When they improve, performance becomes more resilient. When they degrade, the organisation becomes brittle. A Strategic CFO uses these signals to adjust not only numbers, but leadership rhythm.

Common Pitfalls

There are predictable failures in culture-aligned budgeting. Values theatre occurs when culture is discussed, but budgets do not change. Token funding occurs when small line items signal care without changing lived experience. Punitive variance culture teaches people to hide reality, which weakens forecasting and control. Uneven sacrifice collapses trust because people experience the system as unfair. And Finance as enforcer turns budget owners into negotiators rather than leaders.

Each pitfall has the same cure: credibility. Credibility is built through consistent rules, transparent trade-offs, and dignity in delivery. When people trust the process, they stop gaming the numbers. When they stop gaming the numbers, you gain the one resource every CFO needs most: truth, early enough to act.

Final Thought

Budgeting is not just about controlling cost. It is about shaping belief. What you fund, people feel. What you repeatedly defund, they eventually stop believing in. The Strategic CFO leads not only with clarity, but with conscience, ensuring that every line item serves not only performance, but also people, purpose, and possibility.

Because culture is not an abstract concept. Culture is the experience of what happens when pressure arrives. And budgeting is where that pressure becomes visible.

Chapter 7: Building Dashboards That Drive Action

Templates for dashboard architecture and KPI governance are consolidated in Appendix D – Governance & Dashboard Templates.

Turning Metrics into Movement

A dashboard can be a window, or a wall.

It can illuminate insight, reveal drift early, and guide leaders toward the next best decision. Or it can overwhelm with noise, bury responsibility under endless graphs, and give the organisation the illusion of control while momentum quietly leaks away.

The role of the Strategic CFO is not simply to generate dashboards. It is to build decision engines: systems of financial visibility that empower action, not just observation. Because a metric that does not spark movement is not intelligence, it is decoration.

Most organisations do not suffer from a lack of data. They suffer from a lack of interpretability. Leaders are surrounded by information, but uncertain where to look, what matters most, and what must be done now. In that environment, dashboards become screensavers: impressive, polished, and passive.

Your work in this chapter is to turn dashboards into operational instruments. Not "reporting." Not "analytics." Instruments. Something that changes behaviour, accelerates response, and improves the quality of leadership conversations.

Dashboards Are Not Just Reports

Reports say, "Here is what happened." They are backward facing by nature, often delivered too late to influence the outcome. Reports are essential for governance and accountability, but they do not create speed by themselves.

Dashboards should say, "Here is what to do." They are not merely information displays; they are prioritisation systems. Their value is not in volume, but in timing, clarity, and decision linkage.

A high-performing dashboard environment is typically near real-time or at least operationally current. It is action-oriented, designed around what leaders must decide and when. It is tailored to the decision-maker, visually intuitive, and narratively clear. It does not assume the audience speaks fluent finance. It respects the cognitive load of executives and builds meaning into the design.

This is where finance becomes operational, where strategy meets speed, and where numbers are seen not as data, but as decisions waiting to be made.

Executive Case Insight: The Dashboard Everyone Loved, Until It Was Needed

It is common to see dashboards launched with enthusiasm. The design looks elegant. The KPIs are familiar. Leadership nods. Teams attend a walkthrough. The CFO feels progress.

Then volatility hits.

Sales softens unexpectedly. Costs rise. A key region underperforms. Customer churn spikes. Suddenly, the dashboard becomes the centre of attention, and that is when its true quality is revealed.

If the dashboard only shows lag indicators, it will confirm the problem after it is already expensive. If it shows metrics without thresholds, leaders will argue about whether action is needed. If it shows numbers without drivers, departments will defend rather than diagnose. If it shows performance without ownership, responsibility will blur and escalation will stall.

This is the real test: when pressure arrives, does the dashboard reduce debate and accelerate response, or does it create more noise?

The Strategic CFO designs dashboards for pressure, not for presentation.

Step 1: Define the Purpose Before the Platform

Before you touch Power BI, Tableau, Excel, or any other tool, define the purpose with discipline. Tools do not create clarity. Purpose creates clarity.

Ask the questions that matter: What decisions are being made too late today? What do our leaders need to know earlier? What questions do they repeatedly ask in meetings because the current reporting does not answer them? Who is the audience for this dashboard, and what authority do they hold? What actions should this dashboard enable, escalation, reallocation, intervention, reprioritisation, or reinforcement?

A dashboard without purpose becomes a vanity display of green KPIs and irrelevant graphs. It looks "healthy" until it quietly fails the organisation by directing attention away from what matters.

A useful discipline here is to write a one-line purpose statement for every dashboard, such as:

- "This dashboard exists to help the executive team detect revenue risk early enough to intervene within the quarter."
- "This dashboard exists to help operational leaders identify cost drift weekly and correct it before month-end."

- "This dashboard exists to help commercial leadership see pipeline quality and conversion friction in time to change behaviour."

If you cannot articulate the purpose in a single line, the dashboard is not yet ready to be built.

Step 2: Design by Decision, Not by Department

Most dashboards fail because they mirror the org chart rather than the way decisions are made. They become departmental galleries: Sales dashboards for Sales, Operations dashboards for Operations, Finance dashboards for Finance, each optimised for local reporting rather than enterprise action.

But leadership decisions rarely follow departmental boundaries. Decisions follow flows: the movement of value through the enterprise. That means dashboard design must follow the flow of decision-making, not the hierarchy of reporting lines.

Design around strategic themes such as growth, margin, resilience, retention, cash conversion, capacity, and productivity. Design around cross-functional flows such as sales-to-cash, procure-to-pay, hire-to-retire, plan-to-produce, and incident-to-resolution. Design around operational timeframes: daily, weekly, monthly, because different decisions require different cadence. Design around trigger points: if churn rises above a defined threshold, Marketing and Customer Success are alerted; if inventory days exceed a band, Operations and Finance are aligned on intervention; if pipeline coverage drops, Sales leadership escalates corrective action.

The purpose is not to report everything. The purpose is to prioritise attention.

A useful principle is this: one dashboard per decision-maker is better than one dashboard per department. Executives do not need every metric. They need the right metrics, organised in a way that aligns to the decisions they make.

The Decision Engine Model: Signal, Sense, Decide, Act

A dashboard becomes a decision engine when it follows a predictable logic. One effective model is:

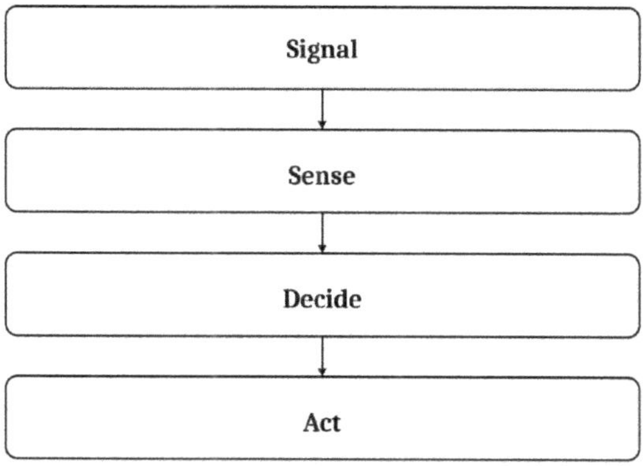

Figure 5 — Decision Engine

Signal: What has changed that requires attention?

Sense: What is driving that change?

Decide: What options are available, and what trade-offs do they carry?

Act: What action is required now, and who owns it?

Most dashboards stop at signal. They show trends and numbers. Dashboards carry the viewer into sense and decision, and they make action unmistakable.

This does not mean your dashboard must contain the entire analysis. It means it must guide the leader to the next step without forcing them to search for meaning. When the dashboard triggers a question, it should also indicate where the answer lives, whether in drill-down, commentary, or a linked driver view.

Step 3: Curate Metrics That Matter

It is tempting to include every available metric. Resist. Dashboards become powerful through curation, not accumulation.

Great dashboards focus on the few metrics that genuinely shape behaviour and outcomes. They include both lead indicators (what is coming) and lag indicators (what already happened). They show thresholds and trends, not just snapshots. They point to root causes, not only symptoms.

For each KPI, ask four questions:

Why does this matter? What decision does it inform? What threshold triggers action? What behaviour are we encouraging by tracking this?

If you cannot answer these questions, the KPI may be interesting but not useful.

A practical way to think about dashboard layers is to build from early signals to strategic outcomes. For example: customer onboarding time (lead indicator) can predict retention issues; net retention rate (lag indicator) confirms the outcome; an operational trigger such as CSAT dropping below a threshold for two consecutive weeks signals immediate attention; a strategic signal such as cost-to-serve by segment reveals whether growth is creating value or destroying margin.

Effective KPI design connects performance measures to clear thresholds and early-warning signals. A dashboard should do more than report what has already happened; it should surface emerging risk early enough for leaders to interpret, escalate, and act before failure compounds.

The KPI Contract: Ownership, Threshold, and Response

A mature dashboard environment treats each KPI as a contract, not a number. Every KPI should have three things attached:

Ownership: Who is accountable for responding when this metric moves?

Threshold: What constitutes "normal," "watch," and "act now"?

Response: What happens when the threshold is crossed?

Without this, dashboards create debate instead of action. Leaders argue about meaning, dispute the severity, or assume someone else is handling it.

When a KPI contract exists, the dashboard becomes an operational system. People know what it means and what to do. It reduces the cost of hesitation.

Step 4: Structure for Interpretation

Every dashboard should help the viewer answer three questions quickly:

1. What is happening?
2. Why is it happening?
3. What should we do?

This is interpretation design. And it is the difference between "data" and "decision."

Use clear headings that match how leaders think: "Revenue vs Forecast, Q2," "Margin Bridge, Drivers," "Cash Conversion, Trend and Risk," "Cost Drift, Exceptions," "Pipeline Quality, Coverage and Conversion."

Use visual signals sparingly and meaningfully. Red and green alone are not enough. Executives need context: what changed, how fast, and why it matters now. If you use colour, it must reflect thresholds that are defined and agreed, not subjective design choices.

Provide context in the dashboard itself, not only in a separate commentary document. Small context cues can transform usability: short annotation boxes, tooltips, or a "What changed this week?" panel that translates movement into narrative.

Enable drill-down for those who want depth, but do not force drill-down to find basic meaning. A smart non-finance leader should be able to interpret the headline story without being trained as an analyst.

This is a crucial CFO mindset: build dashboards for the intelligent non-specialist. Because most decision-makers are not finance professionals. They are operational leaders with limited time who need clarity without friction.

The CFO's Discipline: Fewer Charts, More Meaning

Dashboards are often overdesigned. Too many charts, too many panels, too many competing messages. The viewer does not know where to look first.

A strong discipline is to create a "first view" that is almost austere: a small set of signals that tells the leader what matters today. Then allow depth through drill-down or secondary pages.

If leaders must ask, "What am I looking at?" the design has failed. If leaders can say, "I see the risk, I see the driver, I know what to do next," the design has succeeded.

Step 5: Embed Dashboards Into Leadership Rhythms

A dashboard that is opened only during month-end reviews is not a dashboard. It is a delayed report wearing modern clothing.

Dashboards drive action only when they are embedded into leadership rhythms. That means the dashboard is used in weekly tactical meetings, operational stand-ups, cross-functional reviews, and executive steering sessions. It becomes part of how leadership talks, not an extra artefact that sits on the side.

Embedding requires three things:

First, meeting design must reference the dashboard. The dashboard should not be "an attachment." It should be the agenda. Leaders should review exceptions, discuss drivers, decide actions, and assign owners within the rhythm of the meeting.

Second, threshold alerts must exist for critical changes. Dashboards should not rely on someone remembering to open them. If a key metric crosses a defined band, the responsible leaders should be notified with clarity: what changed, what threshold was crossed, and where to look next.

Third, onboarding must include dashboard fluency. When managers enter the organisation, they should be taught not only what is tracked, but how to use it: how to interpret variance, how to escalate, how to connect metrics to decisions. This transforms dashboards from "Finance reporting" into "enterprise language."

A simple executive move is to run dashboard walkthroughs as part of manager onboarding. When new leaders learn the dashboard rhythm early, they adopt it as normal.

Dashboard Governance: Trust is a Maintenance Discipline

Dashboards fail when they are treated as one-time builds. Dashboards are living systems. They require governance, not to restrict, but to preserve integrity.

Governance means:

- Data definitions are consistent and documented.
- Metric owners are known and accountable.
- Refresh cadence is reliable and communicated.
- Changes to KPI definitions are controlled and transparent.
- The dashboard has a clear lifecycle: build, validate, embed, review, refine.

Trust is not created by design alone. Trust is created by consistency over time.

If the same metric shows different values in different meetings, adoption collapses. If refresh timing is unpredictable, leaders stop relying on it. If KPI definitions drift without communication, departments stop believing the system.

The CFO's role is to treat dashboard trust like financial control: a discipline that is sustained, not a project that is completed.

Common Pitfalls

There are predictable traps that reduce dashboard effectiveness.

Too much data, too little meaning. When leaders must ask what a chart means, the design is not doing its job.

One-size-fits-all design. Executives, operational leaders, and analysts do not need the same view. Tailor dashboards to decision authority and time horizon.

Static dashboards. Outdated data erodes trust quickly. Automate refreshes where possible and communicate cadence clearly.

Design without narrative. A dashboard without context is noise. Meaning must be built into the view through structure, thresholds, and interpretation cues.

Tracking without conversation. Metrics must spark meetings, interventions, and decisions, not simply exist on a screen. A dashboard is only useful when it changes how people lead.

Dashboard Cost: Treat the Information Layer as a Product

A dashboard has a cost structure even when the licence already exists. Every metric requires definition, source maintenance, refresh logic, exception handling, access governance, and someone who answers when the number stops reconciling. The visible screen is the cheapest part. The operating cost sits behind it.

This changes the CFO question from "Can we build it?" to "Is this view valuable enough to maintain?" A useful dashboard should have an owner, a decision purpose, a refresh expectation, and a retirement test. If no decision changes when the metric moves, the metric is decoration. If no one owns the definition, it is future reconciliation work. If the refresh burden exceeds the value of the decision it supports, the architecture is too expensive.

Treat dashboard portfolios the way you treat application portfolios. Review them periodically. Remove duplicate views. Consolidate measures that answer the same question. Track manual interventions, refresh failures, reconciliation hours, and the number of bespoke exports required to make a meeting work. These are maintenance signals. A dashboard that requires a private spreadsheet every month is not functioning as the shared decision surface it claims to be.

The strongest discipline is subtraction. When a new metric is added, ask whether another should leave. This protects executive attention and keeps the semantic layer governable. A smaller dashboard that is trusted, current, and connected to action is more valuable than a comprehensive dashboard that no one can explain.

Executive View and Operator View: One Truth, Different Resolution

Executives and operators should not receive identical dashboards. They should receive different resolutions of the same governed reality. The executive view is designed for orientation and choice: a small set of outcome signals, material drivers, threshold breaches, and decisions that require attention. The operator view is designed for intervention: more granular drivers, workflow measures, queues, cohorts, sites, products, or process stages that show where action can be taken.

The danger is building two truths rather than two resolutions. If the executive dashboard calculates margin one way and the operational dashboard calculates it another, the organisation spends meeting time reconciling language rather than deciding. Both views therefore need to inherit the same definition register, source logic, ownership, and refresh discipline. The difference should be granularity, not meaning.

A practical architecture is to move from outcome to driver to action. The executive sees that conversion is below threshold. The commercial leader can open the driver layer and see whether the cause sits in pipeline quality, stage velocity, pricing, capacity, or churn. The operating team can then move into the action layer where individual queues and tasks live. Each level answers a different question while preserving one chain of causality.

This is also a design test for board reporting. A board should not need the operating dashboard to understand whether the enterprise is inside or outside its governing boundaries. The board view should make the thesis, risk, cash, trajectory, and decision requirements clear. Detail remains available, but it does not lead.

When Two Dashboards Disagree

Two dashboards will eventually disagree. The mature response is neither to choose the prettier one nor to ask Finance to "make the numbers match" before the next meeting. Treat disagreement as a governance event. Pause interpretation, identify the metric and period in dispute, trace both calculations to their source and transformation logic, and establish which definition is authoritative.

Then classify the cause. Definition conflict means the organisation has two meanings for the same label. Source conflict means the views are reading different systems or refresh times. Transformation conflict means filters, joins, allocations, or calculations differ. Timing conflict means one view is current and the other is stale. Ownership conflict means no one has the authority to resolve the difference. Each cause has a different remedy.

Once resolved, publish the decision. Update the definition register, correct the affected views, record whether historical periods require restatement, and communicate the change to the rooms that use the metric. Do not let reconciliation remain private analyst knowledge. Otherwise the same disagreement returns three months later wearing a different label.

Generated commentary adds one more risk. AI can produce fluent explanations of a dashboard before the underlying metric has been reconciled. The prose may sound authoritative while inheriting stale data, a disputed definition, or an incorrect causal inference. The governance rule is therefore explicit: generated commentary never outranks the governed metric and never closes a variance without a human owner. Use AI to accelerate hypothesis generation and drafting, but require the responsible leader to confirm the data, the explanation, and the action before the narrative enters an executive pack.

Final Thought

A dashboard is not a decoration. It is a leadership tool, one that either clarifies reality or hides it.

When you build dashboards that empower action, you do more than track performance. You shape momentum. You create a shared language for decision-making. You reduce the cost of hesitation. You give the organisation the ability to see clearly and respond early, which is one of the rarest competitive advantages in a fast-moving world.

Because the advantage does not go to those who know the most.

It goes to those who see clearly, and act quickly.

That is what you are building now.

Chapter 8: Governance and Accountability

Templates for governance design, escalation, and dashboard control are consolidated in Appendix D – Governance & Dashboard Templates.

Ensuring Clarity, Control, and Commitment at Every Level

Transformation doesn't fail because of bad strategy.

It fails because no one knows who is responsible, what has been decided, and what "good" looks like.

In the modern enterprise, the work is cross-functional, the systems are interconnected, and decisions are made under time pressure. In that environment, ambiguity becomes a silent operational tax. It shows up as delayed approvals, duplicated work, unresolved risks, inconsistent definitions, and performance debates that are really ownership debates. It shows up as leadership fatigue, because every meeting becomes a re-argument of the same fundamentals. It shows up as mistrust, because when the rules are unclear, people assume the worst.

Governance and accountability are not bureaucracy. They are the structure that sustains momentum, prevents chaos, and protects trust. They are the mechanism through which strategy becomes executable and repeatable. When governance is missing, execution becomes personal. When governance is strong, execution becomes institutional.

As CFO, you are not only orchestrating tools and timelines. You are designing the framework that holds the system together. You are setting the rules that determine whether clarity flows or friction multiplies. Governance, at its best, does not slow an organisation down. It speeds it up, because it reduces the cost of uncertainty.

Why Governance Matters More Than Ever

In a fast-changing world, budgets are co-owned. Systems touch every department. Forecasts evolve monthly. Cost centres span geographies. Dashboards are used by leaders who interpret the same number through different lenses. When the enterprise runs on shared systems, it must also run on shared rules.

Without governance, ownership becomes blurred. Mistakes go unreported because people do not know who should act. Approvals get delayed because sign-off pathways are unclear. Accountability becomes a game of pass-the-parcel, where responsibility moves around the table until time runs out and the decision is made by default.

The damage is not only operational. It is cultural. A governance vacuum creates two predictable behaviours. Some people freeze, because they do not want to make the wrong decision. Others act unilaterally, because they cannot wait. Both behaviours weaken alignment, and both force Finance into a late-stage policing role. That role is corrosive. It turns Finance into the blocker, even when Finance is trying to protect the enterprise.

Your role is to create a structure where people know what is expected, decisions are escalated clearly, performance is tracked consistently, and integrity is protected, even under pressure. Integrity is the keyword. Not moral integrity alone, but system integrity: data integrity, process integrity, decision integrity. When integrity is weak, organisations become reactive. When integrity is strong, organisations become confident.

The CFO's Governance Mandate: Make Responsibility Visible

The purpose of governance is to make responsibility visible. Visibility prevents drift. It reduces politics. It stops leadership from discovering too late that no one owned a critical decision. It allows teams to act without hesitation because they know the boundaries, the thresholds, and the escalation path.

In organisations, governance is not a series of committees. It is an operating system. It answers five questions with discipline:

1) Who owns the decision?

2) Who must be consulted before it is made?

3) What information is required to decide well?

4) What triggers escalation or re-opening?

5) How will we know whether the decision is working?

When CFOs lead governance well, the enterprise gains a rare advantage. It becomes easier to make hard decisions quickly, without drama, and without reputational damage. That is not administrative excellence. That is strategic power.

Trust Framework: Clarity, Cadence, and Consequence

Governance works when it is designed around trust. Trust is not a soft concept. It is an execution asset. When trust is high, people act on information quickly. When trust is low, they debate, delay, and seek protection.

A practical trust framework has three pillars.

Clarity: People understand what to do, what the rules are, and what "good" looks like. Clarity is created through decision rights, definitions, and visible ownership.

Cadence: The organisation knows when decisions are made, when performance is reviewed, and when issues are escalated. Cadence reduces emotional volatility because it replaces surprise with rhythm.

Consequence: Not punishment, but follow-through. When governance is real, decisions have owners, owners have obligations, and drift has a response. Consequence is what separates governance from theatre.

If you design governance that delivers these three pillars, you will feel the change immediately. Meetings become shorter. Debates become sharper. Forecast cycles become faster. People stop arguing about whether Finance is "being difficult," because the rules are no longer personal. They are institutional.

Step 1: Define Clear Roles and Accountability Without Creating a Paper Empire

Most organisations do not lack roles. They lack role clarity. Titles exist, but responsibility is blurred. The result is predictable: everyone is involved, and no one is accountable.

The RACI model is useful because it forces explicit answers. But the RACI grid itself is not the transformation. The value lies in the clarity it forces. A governance-ready CFO uses RACI to clarify the high-friction zones, not to document everything in the company.

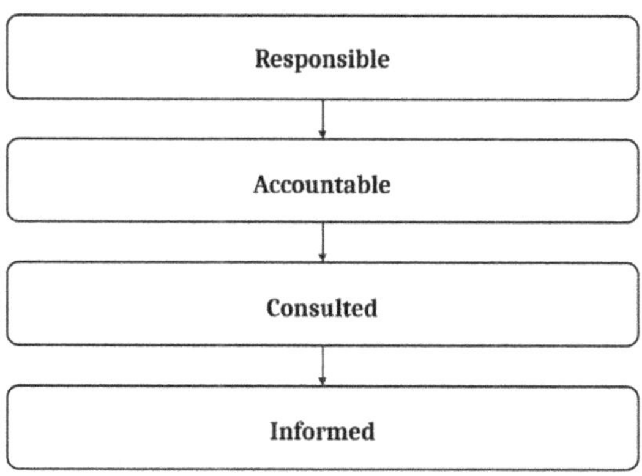

Figure 6 — Decision-right flow

Start where ambiguity is expensive:

budget guidance and target-setting; forecast revisions and scenario changes; cost centre changes and allocation logic; system ownership and master data governance; KPI definitions and dashboard change control; and investment, headcount, and pricing approvals.

Make one executive decision: the “A” role must be singular. If you have multiple accountable parties, you have none. If you have endless consulted stakeholders, you have slowed the system down. Clarity is not created by inclusion. It is created by commitment.

A second decision: define accountability as ownership of outcome, not ownership of tasks. In transformation work, tasks can be delegated. Outcomes cannot.

Step 2: The Decision Rights Map, Written as an Operating Doctrine

The most powerful governance tool is the decision rights map. It is the logic of who decides what, at what thresholds, with what escalation rules. In many organisations, it lives informally. It is known by a few senior people and guessed by everyone else. That is why approvals feel political and inconsistent.

A decision rights map can be expressed in four tiers, creating a doctrine leaders can speak, apply, and enforce.

Tier 1: Operational decisions that leaders can make inside agreed limits. These include routine spend within budget, minor reallocations within a cost centre, and operational trade-offs that do not change enterprise risk. The rule is speed. If leaders cannot decide at Tier 1, the organisation is already slow.

Tier 2: Cross-functional decisions that affect multiple teams or change the agreed plan. These include shifting budget between functions, changing capacity assumptions, or altering the drivers that sit behind the forecast. The rule is alignment. Decisions must be made with the right stakeholders present, and the outputs must be logged.

Tier 3: Executive decisions that materially change the plan, risk posture, or performance trajectory. These include major headcount changes, capex commitments above a set threshold, material changes to pricing strategy, or a reforecast that signals a different year-end outcome. The rule is clarity of trade-offs. These decisions are not "yes or no." They are portfolio choices.

Tier 4: Board-visible decisions that affect covenant, liquidity, capital structure, reputational exposure, or strategy integrity. These include raising or restructuring capital, material acquisitions or divestments, covenant risk, or significant shifts in strategic direction. The rule is confidence. The board must see not only what you decided, but why, and what you will do if assumptions fail.

Once the tiers are clear, you can state the two rules that make decision rights real.

Rule one: A decision is not made until it is written. "Written" does not mean a long memo. It means a decision log entry: what was decided, who owns it, what assumptions it rests on, and what triggers a review.

Rule two: Decisions are reopened only when drivers move materially. Reopening decisions because someone feels anxious is how governance collapses. Reopening decisions because reality changed is how governance stays adaptive.

Decision Rights in Practice: Five Decision Arenas CFOs Must Govern

Decision rights become tangible when you attach them to real decision arenas. In finance transformations, five arenas repeatedly create friction if they are not governed explicitly.

Arena one is spend and reallocation. Most organisations can approve budgets but struggle to make reallocations without conflict. The governance rule is to define what can be moved within a function, what requires cross-functional alignment, and what requires executive approval. A small rule makes a large difference: reallocations that do not change strategic outcomes can be decided at Tier 1 or Tier 2; reallocations that change outcomes require Tier 3 clarity of trade-offs.

Arena two is headcount. Headcount is rarely a simple cost decision. It affects capacity, delivery, morale, and strategic priorities. Governance should define who can approve replacements, who can approve new roles, and what evidence is required to add or freeze hiring. In stable conditions, headcount governance can sit inside light governance. In volatility, it moves into heavy governance, because headcount is one of the fastest ways to alter runway and operational resilience.

Arena three is pricing and commercial terms. Finance is not the owner of commercial strategy, but CFO governance is essential because pricing changes margin, cash conversion, and risk exposure. A decision rights doctrine should define what commercial leaders can do within guardrails, and what requires executive review. Guardrails might include discount thresholds, payment term limits, and approval for non-standard clauses that increase credit risk.

Arena four is capital allocation. Capex, major technology spends, and strategic investment programmes need governance that protects both speed and discipline. The governance principle is to separate “authorisation to explore” from “authorisation to commit.” Too many organisations treat the first business case discussion as the decision. CFOs create a staged gate: permission to analyse, permission to pilot, permission to scale. This keeps the enterprise moving without prematurely locking in commitments.

Arena five is forecast and plan changes. The forecast is not a spreadsheet. It is a contract between leadership and reality. Governance must define who can change drivers, when the forecast is refreshed, and what constitutes a material change that requires executive visibility. Without this, the organisation slides into a negotiation culture where forecast numbers drift based on optimism, defensiveness, or politics. With governance, the forecast becomes an instrument of truth and action.

Escalation Systems: The Difference Between Speed and Chaos

Most governance failures are escalation failures. Either issues are escalated too late, when damage is already done, or escalated too early, creating constant executive noise. An escalation system must therefore be designed with intention.

A practical escalation system has three layers.

Layer one is local escalation. The issue is raised within the function or project team, with a clear request: decision, resource, or clarification. Local escalation should be time boxed. If it cannot be resolved within a defined period, it moves.

Layer two is cross-functional escalation. This is where competing priorities, shared dependencies, or definition conflicts are resolved. The CFO often plays a facilitation role here, ensuring trade-offs are explicit and decisions are written.

Layer three is executive escalation. This is reserved for material risk, material resource conflict, or decisions that change outcomes. The executive escalation rule is simple: escalate with options, not problems. Bring the trade-offs, the recommended path, and the triggers that would cause you to revisit the decision.

A CFO also designs "escalation safety." People must feel safe raising issues early. If escalation is punished, problems go underground. If escalation is welcomed and acted on, the organisation becomes antifragile. One of the most powerful signals a CFO can send is to reward early risk identification, especially when it creates discomfort. That is how trust compounds.

The Reopen Rule: How to Prevent Decision Drift

In transformation work, decision drift is more damaging than a wrong decision. Drift creates perpetual uncertainty and destroys adoption. This is why the reopen rule matters.

A strong reopen rule has two parts. First, a decision can be revisited only when the driver changes materially. Second, the trigger for material change is defined in advance. This prevents the organisation from reopening decisions based on emotion, politics, or convenience. It also protects leaders from feeling that every decision is a personal battle. The rule is not rigid. It is stabilising.

You can make this practical with one phrase: "We reopen on evidence, not on anxiety." When that phrase becomes cultural, governance becomes a performance asset.

Governance as a Confidence Signal During Transformation

During system rollouts, budgeting reforms, and cost structure redesign, governance does something subtle. It signals competence. When leaders see that responsibilities are clear, thresholds are defined, and escalations are disciplined, they relax. They stop worrying that transformation will devolve into chaos. They start believing it can be delivered.

This is why governance is one of the most executive-facing domains of the CFO role. It is where boards and CEOs recognise maturity. Not because governance is complex, but because it is calm, clear, and enforceable.

Step 3: Governance Intensity by Volatility: Light and Heavy Regimes

Governance should not feel the same in every environment. If you govern a stable business like it is in crisis, you will create drag. If you govern a volatile business like it is stable, you will create chaos.

CFOs design governance in two regimes.

Light governance is built for stability. It assumes operating conditions are broadly predictable and the main risk is drift, not collapse. In light governance, cadence is steady: monthly performance reviews, quarterly reforecasts, and clear delegated authority within budget. Escalation is used sparingly, and the system's primary goal is efficiency.

Heavy governance is built for volatility. It assumes operating conditions can change rapidly and the main risk is being late. In heavy governance, cadence tightens rolling forecasts, more frequent liquidity reviews, and quicker escalation. Decision logs become more active, trigger thresholds are explicit, and the Steering Group meets more often.

The critical sophistication is not that you have heavy governance. It is that you can switch between regimes deliberately.

Create a simple volatility trigger doctrine. For example, shift to heavy governance when one or more of the following occurs:

Revenue variance exceeds a defined per cent threshold for two consecutive cycles; cash runway falls below a defined number of weeks or months; a supply disruption or regulatory event introduces material uncertainty; customer churn, conversion, or pipeline health crosses a threshold band; and forecast accuracy deteriorates beyond a defined tolerance.

In heavy governance, you are not "controlling more." You are sensing faster. Heavy governance is an early-warning system with a response mechanism. When the environment stabilises, you return to light governance. That is how you avoid permanent crisis posture.

Step 4: The Executive Steering Group Operating Model

For major transformations, the Steering Group is your governance engine. It is not an update meeting. It is a decision body that protects momentum and trust.

A high-performing Steering Group has five design features.

First, a clear charter. The group exists to make decisions, remove blockers, govern definitions, and protect the programme narrative. It does not exist to review every detail.

Second, the right membership. It must be small enough to act, senior enough to decide, and cross-functional enough to represent the enterprise. Typical members: CFO (chair), transformation lead, CIO or systems owner, HR partner, and one or two business leaders who control the relevant execution environment.

Third, a cadence matched to risk. In stable phases, meet monthly. In volatile phases, meet fortnightly. During go-live windows, meet weekly. Governance is a rhythm, not a calendar appointment.

Fourth, standard artefacts. Every meeting should operate from the same four inputs:

Milestone status (what is on track, what is slipping); risk register (top risks, mitigation, early warnings); decision queue (what needs a decision now); and adoption signals (behaviour, usage, and friction points).

Fifth, disciplined outputs. Every meeting end with three outputs:

1) decisions made today, with owners and timelines

2) actions assigned, with measurable deliverables

3) communications required, and who will deliver them

The Steering Group should also maintain a decision log and a definition register. The decision log prevents institutional amnesia. The definition register prevents metrics and models from drifting quietly into incoherence.

The CFO's personal role in the Steering Group is not to dominate the room. It is to hold the line on integrity and cadence. You are the architect of coherence. That is what the enterprise needs from you.

Operating the Steering Group Like a Decision Machine

A Steering Group becomes powerful when it is treated as an operating mechanism, not a forum. Two small disciplines elevate it.

The first is pre-reads. Send the decision queue and the risk register at least twenty-four hours in advance. If executives see the decision in advance, the meeting becomes a decision moment rather than a discovery moment. The second is the decision record. Each decision is written during the meeting, not after it, and circulated within hours. This prevents post-meeting reinterpretation, which is one of the most common sources of drift.

A useful meeting pattern is the "twenty-minute rule." If a topic cannot be resolved within twenty minutes, it either requires a smaller working group to return with options, or it is an executive decision that needs clearer trade-offs. This keeps governance from becoming endless discussion and protects the organisation's energy.

KPI Governance as Data Lineage and Narrative Discipline

KPIs fail when leaders do not know where the number comes from, how it is calculated, or what changed. This is why KPI governance must include data lineage and narrative discipline.

Data lineage is simple: you can trace the KPI back to its source systems, transformations, and refresh cadence. Narrative discipline is equally simple: every KPI that matters has a standard explanation pattern. What changed, why it changed, and what we will do next. When leaders receive KPIs in that format repeatedly, performance conversations become faster and more constructive.

A high-signal practice is to define “confidence bands” for critical KPIs. Rather than pretending every metric is exact, you define what is reliable, what is estimated, and what is under investigation. This is especially useful during system transitions and volatile periods. Transparency builds trust faster than perfection.

Board Interface Governance as a Contract of Visibility

The board interface should be treated as a contract: what the board will see, how often it will see it, and what it can rely on. The contract should prevent two extremes. Boards should not be surprised by material risk, and they should not be forced into operational detail.

A board-ready governance pack typically includes:

A short performance signal, linked to strategic priorities; a cash and liquidity signal, with runway and headroom; a risk and controls signal, with mitigations and triggers; and a decision and change log, showing what moved since the last board.

The board also needs "if-then" clarity. If revenue falls, what happens to spend? If runway tightens, what happens to headcount? If forecast confidence drops, what cadence changes? When the board sees that structure, it experiences leadership confidence, not leadership hope.

Governance is therefore a form of executive communication. When you design it well, you reduce board anxiety and increase decision speed at the top. That is one of the most valuable outcomes a CFO can deliver.

Step 5: KPI Ownership Doctrine: Definitions That Do Not Drift

KPI governance is where many organisations collapse into noise. They build dashboards, then slowly lose trust because definitions drift, refresh cycles break, and leaders use the same metric to tell different stories.

A KPI without an owner is not a KPI. It is an argument waiting to happen.

A clean KPI ownership doctrine has four parts.

1) Ownership is split into business ownership and data ownership. The business owner is accountable for the outcome. The data owner is accountable for the definition, lineage, and refresh integrity. For some KPIs, both roles sit in Finance. For most enterprise KPIs, business ownership sits with a functional leader and data ownership sits with Finance or analytics.

2) Every KPI has a definition, a source, a refresh cycle, and an escalation threshold. If any of those are missing, the KPI is not governed. A KPI definition should be short and non-negotiable. It should specify what is included and excluded. This prevents the "metric drift" that turns performance into debate.

3) KPI change control is formal. Definitions cannot change because a quarter becomes uncomfortable. If a KPI changes, the change is logged, the reason is stated, and the impact on comparability is made explicit. This is how you protect integrity and avoid selective reporting.

4) KPI review is embedded into cadence. A KPI that is not reviewed in a leadership rhythm is not a KPI. It is a chart. Governance requires that metrics appear in the meeting where decisions are made, and that owners are expected to act when thresholds are crossed.

A CFO also governs KPI proliferation. Executive dashboards do not need fifty metrics. They need a disciplined set of signals that reflect strategy and trigger action. This is why KPI retirement matters. If a KPI no longer drives a decision, retire it. Clarity increases when you remove noise.

Step 6: Board Interface Governance: What the Board Must See, and What Leadership Must Own

Boards do not want operational detail. They want confidence. They want a coherent story, clear risks, and disciplined controls. They want to know whether the enterprise is being steered.

The CFO is the primary designer of the board interface. That interface is governance. It determines what becomes visible at board level, what stays in leadership cadence, and what is managed operationally.

A practical board interface doctrine has three layers.

Layer one: Board essentials. These are the metrics and narratives the board must see because they relate to capital, risk, strategic integrity, and resilience. Typical essentials include liquidity and runway, covenant headroom, material variances and drivers, major investment commitments, and top risks with mitigations. The board also needs early warning indicators and trigger thresholds. They are not there to micro-manage; they are there to govern risk.

Layer two: Executive leadership detail. This is where the CEO and executive team operate weekly and monthly. It includes driver-level performance, adoption signals for transformation programmes, customer and pipeline health, and the operational levers behind financial outcomes. This layer is too detailed for most boards, but essential for leadership action.

Layer three: Operational execution. This is where departmental dashboards and daily decisions live. It is governed through delegated authority and escalation rules, not through board visibility.

The sophistication is not in showing more. It is in showing the right things at the right level.

A governance move is to use board packs that separate signal from noise. Your board pack should include: a one-page performance signal, a one-page risk and controls signal, and a short decision log of what changed since last time. If the board cannot see what changed, they cannot govern effectively.

Board interface governance also includes the rules of escalation. Define what must be taken to the board and what stays with leadership. For example: any risk to covenant, liquidity, capital access, reputational exposure, or strategic direction is board visible. Routine operational variance is not. This prevents the board from being flooded, and it prevents leadership from hiding material risk.

Step 7: Embedding Governance So It Survives You

Governance is only as strong as the habits that carry it. If governance lives in a few leaders' heads, it will dissolve when those leaders leave. If governance is embedded in cadence, it becomes institutional.

Embed governance in four places.

1) Onboarding. New leaders should be taught how decisions are made, how escalations work, and what the performance rhythm is. Do not assume they will "pick it up." Governance that is not taught becomes informal again.

2) Templates and artefacts. Decision logs, definition registers, and escalation pathways should be simple, visible, and repeatedly used. Complexity kills usage. Usability creates discipline.

3) Leadership rituals. Use dashboards in meetings. Use thresholds to trigger action. Use decision logs to prevent re-argument. Governance is not a document. It is a behaviour pattern.

4) Review and refinement. At least annually, review what is slow, what is unclear, and what is over-governed. Remove controls that no longer protect anything. Tighten controls where risk has grown. Governance should evolve with the enterprise.

The Signature Move: Governance That Can Be Spoken in One Breath

If your governance cannot be explained simply, it cannot be lived consistently. The most effective CFOs can describe the operating rules in one breath: "This is who owns the decision, this is when we review it, this is the evidence we use, and this is what triggers escalation." When that sentence becomes normal language across leadership, governance stops being a document and becomes a shared instinct. That is the point at which accountability becomes cultural rather than enforced.

A Practical Governance Audit: Four Questions to Run Quarterly

Governance becomes real when you audit it. Not through a formal compliance exercise, but through four executive questions you can ask each quarter.

First: where are decisions slowing down? Identify the two or three decision types that routinely miss deadlines and redesign the thresholds or the escalation path.

Second: where are definitions drifting? Look for repeated debates about "what the number means." That is a definition register failure. Fix it quickly and publish the definition.

Third: where are owners overloaded? If the same individuals are accountable for too many outcomes, accountability becomes performative. Reassign ownership so it is sustainable.

Fourth: where are shadow processes re-emerging? If teams are rebuilding spreadsheets, running unofficial trackers, or bypassing the system, governance is signalling mistrust. Treat shadow processes as intelligence. They show you where the operating system is not yet credible.

Run these questions quarterly and governance stays light, useful, and alive. Ignore them and governance becomes either heavy theatre or silent decay.

Common Pitfalls

Too much governance and not enough movement. Overly complex sign offs create bottlenecks and a blame culture. People stop acting and start waiting. Governance must enable speed, not replace it.

Hidden accountability. When ownership is vague, nothing gets done and no one is held. Work becomes everyone's problem and therefore no one's responsibility.

One-time setup never reviewed. Governance decays if it is not refreshed. Old rules accumulate and the system becomes heavy.

Governance without communication. If people do not know the process, it does not exist. It lives in executives' heads and fails at operational level.

Control without purpose. Do not enforce rules for enforcement's sake. Tie controls to reasons: integrity, risk, speed, alignment. When people understand the why, they comply with dignity rather than resentment.

The Audit Committee Interface

The audit committee is where financial integrity, control design, judgement, and emerging risk meet formal oversight. A CFO should not treat that interface as a quarterly reporting obligation. It is a governance channel through which the committee gains confidence that the numbers are reliable, material control weaknesses are visible, management judgement is disciplined, and remediation is moving at an appropriate pace (COSO, 2013).

A strong audit committee pack distinguishes routine assurance from matters that require judgement. Routine assurance covers close quality, significant reconciliations, control performance, audit progress, policy changes, and known deficiencies. Judgement matters include material estimates, unusual transactions, changes in accounting treatment, model risk, data-quality concerns, and any area where management confidence is materially lower than the headline number suggests.

The CFO's role is to surface the issue early enough for governance to be useful. Escalation should occur before a problem becomes a disclosure surprise. The committee needs the fact pattern, management's assessment, the range of plausible outcomes, the control response, the accountable owner, and the date by which the issue returns for review.

What Escalates to the Board, and When

Not every variance belongs at board level. The board interface should be triggered by matters that change the enterprise thesis, threaten governing boundaries, require reserved authority, or materially alter the risk the board believes it has accepted. Typical triggers include liquidity or covenant pressure, a material forecast reset, a significant control failure, capital commitments outside approved parameters, major programme failure, regulatory exposure, or a decision whose downside exceeds management's delegated authority.

Timing matters as much as threshold. The board should hear about a material issue when management has enough information to frame the decision, not only when the analysis is complete. Early escalation can be explicitly provisional: what we know, what we do not yet know, what management has already done, what decision may be required, and when the board will receive the next update. That is stronger governance than waiting for certainty while the decision window closes.

Board reporting under stress should become shorter and more frequent, not larger. Protect a stable spine: liquidity and runway, operating trajectory, critical risks, actions taken, decisions pending, and changes since the last update. The purpose is to preserve a shared fact base while conditions move.

Governance of Model-Produced Numbers

As AI and machine-learning outputs enter finance workflows, accountability cannot be delegated to the model. Every model-produced number that enters a management, audit committee, or board pack must have a named human owner who signs off its fitness for the decision being made. The owner does not need to have built the model, but must understand the source, material assumptions, known limitations, validation status, and circumstances in which the output should not be relied upon.

For high-impact outputs, maintain a simple model register: purpose, owner, provider or model version, data classes used, validation date, material limitations, and required review level. This aligns with the governance and traceability principles in NIST AI RMF and ISO/IEC 42001. The control objective is not to slow useful automation. It is to ensure that speed never creates an accountability vacuum (NIST, 2023; NIST, 2024; ISO/IEC 42001:2023; OECD, 2019).

Final Thought

Governance is not a cage.

It is a scaffold for success.

Accountability is not punishment.

It is permission to lead clearly and confidently.

As CFO, you are the architect of trust. The clearer your systems of decision rights, definitions, and escalation, the more agile, aligned, and resilient your organisation becomes.

When everyone knows the rules, the enterprise moves faster, and the wins come easier, because clarity is no longer negotiated. It is engineered. It keeps the enterprise honest, aligned, and ready to move.

Chapter 9: Financial Orchestration in Crisis & Complexity

Crisis governance, escalation, and decision-right templates are consolidated in Appendix D – Governance & Dashboard Templates.

Leading When the Plan Breaks

No matter how well you budget, structure cost centres, or implement systems, at some point the plan will break.

A crisis will hit.

The forecast will collapse.

A new regulation, a supply shock, a leadership shake-up, or something no model predicted, will enter the picture.

This chapter is about what happens next. Because financial leadership is not tested when things go right. It is revealed when they don't.

In calm markets, CFO excellence is often measured by optimisation: tighter forecasts, cleaner reporting, sharper margin, better dashboards. In crisis, CFO excellence is measured by coherence: how quickly the organisation regains clarity, how intelligently it adapts, and how well it protects trust while making difficult decisions at speed.

Crisis leadership is not heroic improvisation. It is orchestration under pressure, the ability to create a stable decision environment inside an unstable world.

The Nature of Modern Crisis

Today's disruptions are not rare interruptions. They are recurring conditions. They arrive more frequently, more suddenly, and in more complex forms than most legacy planning models were built to handle.

Modern crises are frequent: global and local shocks no longer wait a decade between appearances. They are multi-dimensional: financial, operational, ethical, reputational, often at the same time. They are fast-moving: decisions are needed before certainty arrives. And they are emotionally charged: people look to Finance not only for numbers, but for calm, direction, and credibility (Weick and Sutcliffe, 2007).

In this environment, the CFO is not merely the person who "protects the P&L." The CFO becomes a stabiliser of the enterprise nervous system.

You interpret reality without panic. You reduce noise. You prioritise what matters. You ensure the organisation does not mistake urgency for wisdom.

Your job is not just to hold the line. It is to provide the clarity that allows others to move wisely, even through fog.

Crisis as an Operating Mode, Not an Event

A subtle but important shift has occurred in the executive landscape: crises are no longer isolated events to be "managed and closed." They increasingly become operating modes the organisation must sustain for months, sometimes years, while still delivering performance.

This means two things for the CFO.

First, you must design financial systems that can flex without breaking rolling forecasting capability, fast scenario refresh, and liquidity visibility that can tighten and loosen with conditions.

Second, you must design leadership cadence for uncertainty. In crisis mode, the organisation needs a predictable rhythm of updates, decisions, escalation paths, and truth-telling.

The CFO often becomes the architect of that rhythm because Finance sits at the intersection of operational reality and resource reality.

In crisis, your calm becomes operational infrastructure: it makes truth speakable and action possible again.

Step 1: Shift from Precision to Preparedness

In crisis, traditional models often fail, not because they are mathematically wrong, but because they are built on assumptions that no longer hold.

Many models rely on stability. They assume rational behaviour. They take too long to update. They become dangerous not because they are imperfect, but because they create false confidence.

Strategic CFOs do not aim for perfect predictions in crisis. They build systems that are ready to flex.

Preparedness is superior to precision when volatility dominates.

Preparedness means a rolling forecast updated bi-weekly or monthly, depending on pace.

It means scenario modelling with best-case, base-case, and worst-case logic that can be refreshed quickly as new information arrives.

It means triggers and thresholds that signal when to act, before the organisation is forced into reaction by sudden deterioration.

In a crisis, your role is to help the organisation move from reaction to intention as fast as possible.

Your task is to acknowledge uncertainty without surrendering leadership.

You do not need perfect information to lead. You need a coherent framework for acting under uncertainty, and a consistent method for updating decisions as reality changes (Kahneman, 2011; Weick and Sutcliffe, 2007).

The Two-Speed Finance Doctrine

The CFO's most practical contribution in crisis is to run Finance in two speeds: normal mode and crisis mode.

The problem in many organisations is not that they cannot act fast; it is that they do not know when to switch, and they do not know how to switch without chaos.

Normal mode is built for optimisation. It uses monthly close rhythms, planned reviews, quarterly reforecasting, and structured governance.

Crisis mode is built for survival and optionality. It tightens time horizons, compresses decision cycles, and increases frequency of truth.

Two-speed finance is not a permanent state of alarm. It is a deliberately designed switch that allows the enterprise to tighten and loosen without breaking trust.

The CFO defines the switch criteria in advance where possible and then applies them without drama.

Examples of switch triggers include liquidity runway falling below a defined threshold, a sudden revenue shock, a covenant headroom squeeze, or a material operational interruption.

When you switch to crisis mode, three things must happen immediately.

First, the time horizon shortens from annual budgets to thirteen-week cash focus.

Second, reporting frequency increases: from monthly variance to weekly operating signals.

Third, decision rights tighten: fewer people decide, but everyone understands what is being decided and why.

The First Forty-Eight Hours: A CFO Micro-Playbook

The beginning of a crisis is where organisations either stabilise quickly or enter a spiral of confusion.

The first forty-eight hours are not about solving everything. They are about establishing control of truth.

Begin with three immediate actions.

First, secure cash reality. Confirm bank balances, sweep positions, and payment obligations due within the next fourteen days.

Identify any payment runs, payroll timing, tax dates, and debt service events. Lock the baseline so the organisation stops debating what is real.

Second, set the cadence. Schedule the war-room, set update times, and define the artefacts that will exist after every meeting: updated cash spine, decision log, action register, and risk register.

When the rhythm is set, panic reduces because people know when clarity will arrive.

Third, publish the "rules of crisis mode." Keep them simple.

What needs approval now? What is paused? What is protected? How do teams escalate risks?

The goal is not control; it is coherence. People behave better when they understand the rules.

Complexity Stacks: When the Crisis Has Layers

Some crises are singular events. Many are stacked.

You may face a demand shock while a regulatory change is landing, while a cyber incident disrupts operations, while a leadership transition destabilises confidence.

In layered crisis, the CFO's job is to prevent the organisation from treating every problem as equally urgent.

Use a hierarchy of threats. Protect solvency first. Protect legal compliance second. Protect operational continuity third. Protect strategic positioning fourth.

This hierarchy does not mean ignoring strategy; it means sequencing decisions, so the enterprise survives to execute strategy.

A practical method is to maintain two registers: the immediate register and the strategic register.

The immediate register contains decisions that must be made within seven days.

The strategic register contains decisions that must be revisited within thirty to ninety days, once fog clears.

This prevents long-term choices being made in short-term panic.

Step 2: Activate Your Financial Contingency Plan

If you have built well, you will already have a contingency framework.

If not, now is the time to build one, live, under pressure, with execution rigour.

A crisis contingency plan begins with liquidity visibility.

Everything else is secondary. You cannot protect strategy if you cannot protect solvency.

Start with a cash runway dashboard updated daily or weekly, depending on volatility.

Make it simple, visible, and trusted. If cash visibility becomes disputed, you lose the ability to lead.

Then run a cost elasticity review: what can be paused, renegotiated, reduced, or delayed, and what must remain protected to preserve core capability.

Many organisations cut indiscriminately in crisis and later discover they cut the very muscle needed for recovery.

Next, create a revenue risk map.

Which customers are most vulnerable? Which channels are fragile? Which contracts are exposed to renegotiation? Which revenue streams are resilient?

Do not treat revenue risk as a single number. Treat it as a portfolio with different behaviours under stress.

Then build a capital access plan.

What credit lines exist? What covenant constraints apply? What reserves are available? What investor scenarios are viable?

What would you do if the crisis worsens beyond your base case?

Begin with liquidity.

Then protect operational stability.

Then look for opportunities hidden inside disruption.

Crises do not only destroy value. They also reallocate it, toward those who can adapt faster and act with clarity.

The Thirteen-Week Cash Spine

When crisis arrives, annual budgets become almost irrelevant.

What matters is cash timing, not just cash totals.

The practical backbone of crisis finance is the thirteen-week cash forecast, a living view that tells you, week by week, what is committed, what is likely, and what is discretionary.

The work begins with definitions.

“Committed” means contractual and unavoidable within the horizon: payroll, taxes, debt service, lease obligations, essential utilities, critical supplier payments where non-payment stops operations.

“Likely” means expected inflows and outflows based on current evidence: customer receipts with collection history, expected rebates, forecasted variable spend.

“Discretionary” means levers you can actively pull: capex deferrals, non-essential vendor spend, hiring pauses, travel, and discretionary programmes.

Your forecast must separate those categories.

If it does not, you will misread optionality.

You will assume you can delay what you cannot delay, and you will miss levers you could have used earlier.

The CFO’s job is to make optionality visible.

Build the forecast from bank reality, not accounting timing.

Start with actual bank balances.

Reconcile to the ledger so Finance and Treasury speak the same truth.

Then map inflows and outflows by payment behaviour, not invoice date.

In crisis, assumptions about timing are often more important than assumptions about volume.

Finally, connect the thirteen-week view to trigger bands.

A strong practice is to define three runway bands and pre-agreed actions:

Stability band: runway above a defined threshold, with a focus on monitoring and light tightening; pressure band: runway tightening, activating working capital levers and cost elasticity actions; and threat band: runway below threshold, activating emergency measures and board-level escalation.

Do not treat these bands as fear signals. Treat them as operating signals.

Bands remove drama. They create pre-decision when the threshold is crossed, action feels deliberate rather than panicked.

The Liquidity War-Room Rhythm

A liquidity war-room is not a room; it is a rhythm.

Its purpose is to turn uncertainty into a manageable sequence of decisions.

In crisis mode, the war-room rhythm is often daily for the first two weeks, then three times per week once stability improves.

Keep meetings short and disciplined.

The war-room exists to do four things: update the cash reality, surface new risks, decide immediate actions, and assign owners.

The dashboard is the spine.

It should include starting cash, committed inflows, committed outflows, and discretionary levers.

It should show a thirteen-week view, not a year.

It should be grounded in bank data, not only ERP timing.

And it should clearly separate what is contractual from what is assumed.

The CFO chairs the war-room because the CFO integrates the trade-offs.

But the CFO does not run it alone.

Include the operational owners who can move the levers: Commercial for collections and renewals, Procurement for payment terms, HR for workforce decisions, Operations for inventory and capacity, Legal for contract constraints, and Communications when narrative risk is material.

A simple war-room agenda creates stability:

cash and runway update, material deltas since last meeting, top five risks, top five actions, decisions and escalations, owner check-out with due dates.

If your war-room ends without decisions, it is not a war-room. It is a status meeting.

Working Capital as a Leadership Lever

In many crises, the fastest improvement does not come from "cost cutting."

It comes from working capital orchestration, accelerating cash in, slowing cash out intelligently, and reducing trapped cash in inventory or processes.

Cash-in levers include collections discipline, invoice accuracy, billing frequency, early-payment incentives where commercially sensible, and targeted credit control for high-risk accounts.

The CFO should partner with Commercial to segment receivables: strategic accounts, healthy accounts, watchlist accounts, and high-risk accounts.

Each segment gets a different approach.

Blanket pressure on all customers destroys relationships and rarely increases collections meaningfully.

Cash-out levers include renegotiating terms with suppliers, prioritising payments that protect continuity, and sequencing spend so the enterprise stays operational.

Procurement becomes a cash partner in crisis, not a savings department.

Renegotiations are not only about price; they are about timing, volume flexibility, and termination rights.

Legal should be involved early so that renegotiation does not create hidden risk.

Inventory and production levers matter if your organisation carries stock.

Crisis often exposes where cash is trapped in slow-moving inventory or misaligned purchasing.

Operational decisions that reduce inventory days can release liquidity faster than any executive mandate.

The CFO's role is to quantify those levers and make them decision-ready:

"If we reduce inventory days by X, we release Y cash within Z weeks."

CFOs do not merely report working capital.

They orchestrate it across functions with shared targets, clear owners, and a cadence that makes movement visible.

Step 3: Lead Cross-Functional Decision Rooms

In crisis, silos kill speed.

They create duplication, contradictory narratives, and slow escalations.

The CFO's role is to create one decision room, one shared reality, and one rhythm of action.

Establish a rapid response group that includes the CEO, CFO, Head of People, Operations and Commercial leads, and a communications or risk lead where relevant.

Meet daily or every other day depending on intensity.

Use a shared dashboard that monitors liquidity, customer signals, operational constraints, and key decisions in flight.

Track regulatory or reputational risks alongside financial ones, because reputational damage often becomes financial damage later.

Your superpower as CFO is bringing facts to emotional moments and helping others interpret them without panic.

That does not mean being cold. It means being steady.

It means holding the organisation's decision environment stable when the external environment is unstable.

A decision room must not become reporting theatre.

It must become a place where decisions are made and recorded.

Every meeting should end with clear actions, owners, deadlines, and escalation triggers.

In crisis, clarity is not a luxury. It is operational survival.

Decision Rights Under Pressure

Crisis reveals whether your decision rights are real.

In normal times, organisations can afford ambiguity because time cushions mistakes.

In crisis, ambiguity becomes expensive.

The CFO should establish a decision rights map in narrative form, so it is understood and repeatable.

Who decides on spend freezes and exceptions?

Who decides on price moves, contract concessions, and customer credit?

Who decides on workforce levers, from hiring pauses to restructuring?

Who decides on capex deferrals and vendor renegotiations?

Who decides when the organisation exits crisis mode?

The purpose is not to centralise power for ego. The purpose is to protect speed and integrity.

When decision rights are clear, teams act faster and escalate earlier.

When decision rights are unclear, teams hesitate, and decisions happen through informal negotiation rather than deliberate choice.

CFOs also design exception logic.

In crisis, the organisation will need a fast path for exceptions that protect revenue, safety, or critical capability.

Exceptions should require a short-written rationale, a clear owner, and a post-decision review.

This prevents "exception creep" while allowing the business to keep moving.

Two-Speed Governance

Two-speed finance requires two-speed governance.

In normal mode, governance protects consistency, compliance, and long-term integrity.

In crisis mode, governance protects speed and coherence.

That means reducing approval layers while increasing clarity.

It means narrowing decision forums but widening transparency.

It means tightening definitions and thresholds while loosening non-essential bureaucracy.

A practical move is to define "crisis approvals" as time bound.

For example, spend approvals may be centralised during crisis mode, but only for a defined period, with weekly review.

This prevents temporary discipline turning into permanent control.

The CFO's role is to ensure crisis governance does not become culture damage.

Speed cannot come at the cost of dignity.

The organisation must feel that governance is protection, not punishment.

Step 4: Track What's Failing, and What's Emerging

During disruption, some structures break, and others reveal surprising strength.

A crisis is both a threat and a diagnostic instrument. It shows you what was real and what was theatre.

Use this time to observe the organisation with executive attention.

Which teams adapt fastest, and why?

Which processes still function under pressure, and which collapse?

What costs remain essential when the organisation tightens?

Which reports are ignored, and which become daily staples?

Which leadership behaviours stabilise teams, and which destabilise them?

Crises reveal the truth about capability.

They show whether agility is embedded or merely spoken.

They expose whether dashboards are useful or decorative.

They reveal whether governance is real or performative.

The Strategic CFO captures these truths in real time.

Not as retrospective judgement, but as operating intelligence.

You are watching the organisation's true operating system reveal itself.

That knowledge becomes your blueprint for post-crisis strengthening.

The Crisis Signal Stack

In crisis, the organisation needs a short list of signals that matter more than the rest.

This is not the time for fifty KPIs. It is the time for a signal stack that tells you whether reality is improving or deteriorating.

An effective signal stack usually covers liquidity runway, order intake and conversion, customer payment behaviour, churn or renewal risk, operational capacity constraints, and people risk signals such as attrition spikes or burnout indicators.

Choose signals that move early, not only after damage is done.

Do not only show numbers. Show thresholds.

A signal without a threshold is a statistic.

A signal with a threshold is a trigger.

Triggers remove debate because they pre-define what action is expected when the signal moves.

The Decision Log: Protecting Memory Under Stress

Crisis creates decision amnesia.

Leaders make a hard call, and two weeks later the organisation forgets why it was made.

That is when re-litigation begins, and speed collapses.

Maintain a decision log with three fields: the decision, the rationale, and the revisit date.

The revisit date is essential.

It tells the organisation that decisions are not permanent truths; they are best choices under current information.

When the revisit date arrives, the decision is reassessed calmly.

This practice reduces politics and increases trust.

Step 5: Communicate with Empathy and Discipline

The most dangerous phrase in a financial crisis is, "Let's wait and see."

It sounds cautious, but it signals drift.

It tells people that leadership is watching uncertainty rather than shaping response.

In uncertain environments, people will not wait quietly.

They will fill the silence with fear, speculation, and defensive behaviour.

Instead, communicate early, even if not all answers are known.

Use a calm, clear, confident tone.

Admit uncertainty but explain your method for navigating it.

Frame updates through what is changing, what is staying stable, and what is needed from teams right now.

Your words shape the emotional stability of your organisation, not just their tasks.

This is especially true for Finance.

When Finance disappears in crisis, people assume the worst.

When Finance becomes visible, steady, and human, people feel anchored.

Empathy does not weaken discipline. It strengthens it.

People comply, collaborate, and escalate risk earlier when they feel respected rather than blamed.

The Stakeholder Narrative: One Crisis, Many Audiences

A crisis creates different fears for different stakeholders.

CFOs do not broadcast a single generic message.

They maintain one truth, but they translate it with precision.

For the board, the narrative must be decision-grade.

Boards need a concise view of liquidity, risk exposure, strategic trade-offs, and the decision plan.

They must see what the organisation is doing this week, what the next thresholds are, and what decisions may require board support.

For lenders and investors, the narrative must be credibility focused.

They want evidence of discipline: a clear cash view, covenant headroom logic, concrete levers, and a governance cadence.

They will respond to honesty paired with structure.

They will punish optimism without control.

For employees, the narrative must be human and stabilising.

People need to know what is changing, what is safe, and what is expected.

They also need to feel that leadership is present.

Silence creates rumours.

Over-detail creates panic.

The CFO's tone matters: calm, factual, respectful, and consistent.

For customers and suppliers, the narrative must protect continuity and trust.

Where relevant, communicate proactively about service stability, payment plans, and contract expectations.

In crisis, uncertainty triggers defensive behaviours; proactive clarity reduces churn and renegotiation pressure.

The Covenant and Credibility Play

If your organisation has lenders, crisis introduces a second battlefield: covenant confidence.

Covenant risk is rarely solved by last-minute negotiation.

It is managed by building credibility early.

Start by understanding covenant mechanics, not just covenant thresholds.

What is the measurement date? What definitions apply? What add-backs are permitted?

What cure rights exist? How does a breach trigger cross-defaults or pricing changes?

Who must be notified, and when?

Then build a lender narrative pack.

Keep it concise and disciplined.

It should include current liquidity and runway; the thirteen-week cash spine; scenario view with clear assumptions; the levers already executed; the levers ready to execute; and governance cadence (how often leadership is reviewing, and what escalation thresholds exist).

Lenders respond well to visibility and discipline.

They respond badly to late surprises.

A practical principle: communicate before you need permission.

If you wait until you are in breach, you have already reduced trust.

If you communicate early with a structured plan, you increase the chance of flexibility when you need it.

Board Interface in Crisis

Boards do not want noise. They want decision-grade truth.

The CFO's crisis board interface should be designed as an operating system, not a presentation.

A strong board interface has three layers:

Reality layer: liquidity, runway, performance deltas, material risks, key assumptions that changed.

Decision layer: what leadership decided this week, what decisions are pending, and what trade-offs exist.

Support layer: what leadership needs from the board, approvals, introductions, risk appetite alignment, or strategic permission to act.

Keep the cadence predictable.

In early crisis, weekly board updates may be appropriate; later, bi-weekly or monthly.

The point is not to flood the board.

The point is to maintain shared reality and reduce the chance of late-stage interventions driven by fear.

Commercial and Pricing Levers in Complexity

Not all crises are liquidity crises.

Many are margin crises, demand crises, or confidence crises.

Finance must therefore orchestrate commercial levers as well as cost levers.

In complex disruption, pricing discipline often becomes the hidden differentiator.

Organisations under pressure discount too quickly.

They trade long-term margin for short-term comfort and then discover the market has reset around a lower price point.

The CFO should work with Commercial to define pricing guardrails:

where discounting is permitted, where it is not, what deal structures protect value, and what concessions should be traded for commitment.

In crisis, concessions should buy something:

longer term, faster payment, reduced scope, reduced service cost, or strategic reference value.

Equally important is pipeline truth.

In crisis, forecasts become political.

Leaders want the optimistic number to protect morale.

Finance must protect credibility.

The CFO's role is to separate hope from evidence and to ensure the organisation plans from what is probable, not what is wished.

The Human Stability System

Even a perfect crisis plan fails if the organisation burns out.

Crisis operating mode introduces fatigue, fear, and short decision horizons.

People begin to act defensively.

They stop escalating risks because they assume leadership is already overloaded.

They hoard information.

They become cautious in ways that slow recovery.

The CFO cannot solve morale alone, but the CFO can prevent finance processes from amplifying fear.

One of the most powerful CFO moves is to make the organisation feel that it is being led, not merely observed.

That means keeping a steady cadence.

It means not changing the message every week.

It means acknowledging strain without dramatizing it.

It means protecting a few non-negotiables that keep the organisation human:

clear communication, respectful decision-making, and visible appreciation for those carrying extra load.

Step 6: Recover with Reflection, Not Regression

When the crisis passes, resist the urge to "go back to normal."

Normal may be what failed you.

The point of crisis is not simply survival; it is learning.

Conduct a financial post-mortem.

Capture what you will do differently next time.

Update dashboards, models, governance, and decision rhythms based on what happened in reality, not what was assumed in planning.

Identify investments made under pressure that should now be scaled.

Identify costs cut under fear that should be restored strategically.

Post-crisis fatigue often leads to missed transformation.

Leaders are relieved, exhausted, eager to move on.

But the window immediately after crisis is when organisations have the highest willingness to change systems, because the pain has made the weaknesses undeniable.

Disruption is painful, but it delivers truth. Use it.

The Post-Crisis Reset: What Gets Rewritten, What Gets Codified

A mature CFO treats recovery as a reset programme, not a celebratory return.

Reset means rewriting what was proven weak, and codifying what was proven strong.

Rewrite the forecasting and liquidity architecture.

If cash visibility was slow, build a control tower that can tighten within twenty-four hours.

If scenarios were stale, build a scenario refresh cadence with clear ownership.

If revenue risk was misunderstood, rebuild the portfolio view and leading indicators.

Rewrite decision rights where drift appeared.

If approvals were unclear, codify the decision map.

If escalation was feared, rebuild escalation as support.

If exception logic was abused, redesign the exception pathway and post-decision review.

Codify the war-room rhythm into a reusable playbook.

Your organisation should not have to reinvent calm.

Document the cadence, the dashboard definitions, the meeting agenda, the artefacts produced, and the governance rules.

This is how resilience becomes institutional, not personal.

Codify behavioural disciplines that protected trust.

If weekly updates reduced fear, keep a lighter version in normal times.

If dashboards created speed, embed them in leadership routines permanently.

The goal is to retain the muscle without living in crisis.

Post-Crisis: Returning to Normal Without Losing the Muscle

The exit from crisis mode must be designed.

If you simply stop the war-room, the organisation will drift.

If you keep crisis controls forever, the organisation will suffocate.

Define exit criteria.

What signals tell you that the organisation can loosen?

It may be runway returning above threshold, covenant headroom stabilising, customer churn normalising, supply chain reliability returning, or volatility reducing.

Then design the handover.

Reduce war-room frequency gradually.

Transition from daily cash calls to weekly cash reviews.

Maintain the thirteen-week cash spine but loosen the approval controls around discretionary spend.

Keep the best behavioural disciplines: clean definitions, clear owners, and fast escalation.

The goal is to retain resilience as capability, not as anxiety.

Organisations that learn this become anti-fragile.

They do not merely recover; they improve.

Step 7: Codify Resilience as a Permanent Capability

After the post-crisis reset, the final step is to embed resilience into the normal operating system.

This is how crisis stops being trauma and becomes learning.

Codify the crisis playbook into your finance operating manual.

Build the cash spine as a permanent capability that can be tightened within twenty-four hours.

Maintain a light version of the signal stack in normal times so early warnings are not missed.

Train leaders on the two-speed doctrine so that switching modes feels familiar rather than frightening.

Most importantly, protect the cultural lesson: calm is a strategy.

Organisations that remain coherent under pressure do not do so by accident.

They do so because leaders designed for it and then practiced it until it became normal.

A final executive discipline: separate "fast truth" from "slow truth."

Fast truth is what you must know today to protect runway and continuity.

Slow truth is what you will understand over weeks as data stabilises.

Finance must provide both without confusing them.

When leaders demand certainty too early, give them a range and the triggers that would move it.

When leaders hide uncertainty to appear confident, insist on transparency.

Confidence is not pretending; it is navigating openly.

This is the CFO's quiet advantage in crisis and complexity: you make uncertainty usable.

You translate disruption into decisions, fear into cadence, and chaos into a sequence the organisation can execute.

When that sequence exists, teams stop improvising in isolation.

They escalate earlier.

They collaborate more cleanly.

And the organisation recovers faster, not because the crisis was smaller, but because your orchestration prevented confusion from becoming a second crisis inside the enterprise.

Common Pitfalls

There are predictable errors that compound crisis damage.

Waiting too long to change forecasts: delayed decisions compound harm. Crisis does not wait for tidy data.

Freezing all spend without strategy: panic cuts often destroy capability, morale, and recovery strength.

A silent Finance function: in crisis, Finance must be visible, present, and trusted. Silence creates fear.

Over-reliance on old tools: if your dashboard does not serve you in crisis, rebuild it. Crisis is the ultimate usability test.

Missing the learning moment: if you do not harvest lessons and update your systems, you will relive the same crisis dynamics again, with a different trigger but the same structural weakness.

Final Thought

Crisis does not destroy your finance systems. It reveals what they were built for.

As CFO, you are not the defender of the past.

You are the steward of the organisation's resilience, clarity, and capacity to evolve.

When the plan breaks, you don't.

You steady the system.

You hold the line.

And you lead, not just through the storm, but beyond it.

Chapter 10: The CFO as Builder of Systems, People, and Legacy

Legacy and governance health checks are consolidated in Appendix D – Governance & Dashboard Templates.

The practical templates, checklists, and governance tools referenced across this volume are consolidated in Appendices A–D.

From Project Delivery to Enduring Impact

Numbers change. Systems evolve. Markets shift. But what remains, long after the budget closes, the dashboards refresh, and the forecasts adjust, is the legacy of how you built.

This chapter is not about tools. It is about what endures. Because at the highest level of financial orchestration, you are no longer simply solving problems. You are building foundations that others will stand on, and operating coherence that will outlive your tenure.

The modern CFO is often evaluated through visible outputs: forecast accuracy, margin improvement, cost discipline, faster close, cleaner reporting, board confidence. These matter. But behind those outcomes sits a deeper question that separates competent execution from enduring leadership: will the system you built still produce clarity when you are no longer in the room?

Will the people you developed still lead well when you have moved on? Will the organisation's financial language remain coherent under pressure, or collapse into politics and confusion the moment your presence disappears?

Legacy is not sentiment. Legacy is operational continuity. It is measured in what keeps working when leadership changes. It is measured in whether the next CFO inherits a strengthened system or a fragile one. It is measured in whether the enterprise becomes more capable, more disciplined, and more intelligent because you were there, not merely more optimised for a season.

Legacy Is an Operating System

Executive legacy is often discussed as reputation. CFO legacy is more precise. It is architecture: the decisions, rhythms, definitions, governance, and capabilities that remain after your exit.

If financial performance depends on your personal vigilance, then what you have built is not a system. It is a dependency. The goal of orchestration is to move the enterprise from dependence to durability.

This requires a shift in how you think about your role. You are not only the steward of numbers; you are the steward of how the organisation interprets numbers. You are not only the owner of processes; you are the designer of decision environments.

The difference is subtle, but transformative. A process tells people what to do. A decision environment tells people how to think, what to prioritise, and how to act when reality deviates from plan.

Systems That Outlive You

Many CFOs spend their careers chasing the clean month-end, the streamlined cost model, or the perfect dashboard. Those pursuits are not wrong. But if the system only works because you personally hold it together, then it will weaken the moment you are not present.

The true question is not, "Is this process efficient?" The true question is, "Is this process durable?"

Durability means the system delivers clarity without constant heroic intervention. It means the enterprise can run the rhythm, interpret the outputs, and make decisions with confidence even when the CFO changes, the CEO changes, or the business enters a new market regime.

To build durability, the CFO must design for transfer. The organisation must be able to execute the intent of your work without copying your personality. That is what makes a legacy real.

The Durability Doctrine: Six Tests of a Real System

A durable finance operating system can be tested. When you want to know whether you have built something that will outlive you, apply six tests. If your system fails any of them, it will eventually revert to improvisation.

In practice, this often looks like coherence: the same number means the same thing in every room. Definitions are governed, not negotiated; repeatability: the rhythm can be run without informal knowledge. Cadence, inputs, and outputs are explicit; interpretability: non-finance leaders can understand what they see and what to do next. If the system requires translation every month, it is fragile; escalation safety: risk is raised early because escalation is structured and non-punitive. Silence does not feel safer than honesty; resilience under stress: when volatility rises, the system tightens without breaking. It shifts cadence and thresholds, rather than collapsing into chaos; and auditability: decisions, assumptions, and trade-offs are recorded. When leadership changes, the organisation can see why the present exists.

These tests are not theoretical. They are the practical difference between an enterprise that keeps moving under pressure and one that fragments into debate.

If you want to leave behind something that lasts, you build for these conditions, not for best-case calm.

Rhythms That Stabilise the Enterprise Nervous System

In earlier chapters, we treated cadence as an executive tool: budgeting as organisational rhythm, governance as decision clarity, crisis as two-speed finance. Legacy is built when those rhythms become institutional, not personality driven.

The CFO's rhythms are not administrative. They are stabilisers. They reduce noise. They allow the organisation to detect drift early and respond with composure.

A legacy-grade rhythm usually has three layers:

The performance rhythm: monthly close and performance review that translates numbers into decisions, not explanations; the directional rhythm: rolling forecast and scenario refresh that protects agility without undermining commitments; and the integrity rhythm: governance checkpoints that keep definitions, KPIs, and decision rights coherent.

When these rhythms are consistent, the enterprise becomes harder to destabilise. People know when truth will surface, where decisions will be made, and how uncertainty will be handled. That predictability is not bureaucracy. It is executive calm made structural.

Two-Speed Finance as a Standing Design

Most organisations treat crisis cadence as an exception: a temporary war-room that appears in panic and disappears in relief. A more mature design is to build two-speed finance into the operating system itself.

In stable conditions, the review rhythm is designed for learning and optimisation. In volatile conditions, it is designed for liquidity protection, fast recalibration, and narrative coherence. Your system should be able to switch modes without redesign.

This means codifying the triggers that activate crisis cadence: liquidity thresholds, revenue shock bands, covenant proximity, operational disruption indicators, or regulatory events. It also means codifying what changes and what does not.

What changes is frequency, depth, and escalation paths. What does not change is integrity: one version of the truth, recorded assumptions, and disciplined decision capture.

A CFO who leaves this design behind gives the organisation a rare advantage. The next crisis will still be painful, but it will not be chaotic. The enterprise will know how to shift gears.

Governance as Memory: The Organisation Must Remember What It Decided

One of the most common forms of executive dysfunction is decision amnesia. Leaders decide, but the organisation does not remember. Assumptions are lost. Trade-offs are forgotten. The same debates return every quarter, dressed in slightly different language.

This is not a personality flaw. It is a governance design flaw. Without decision capture, the organisation becomes trapped in repetition.

Legacy-grade governance does not produce more meetings. It produces memory: clear decision rights, explicit thresholds, and recorded rationale.

A practical governance architecture includes:

Decision rights that distinguish between recommendation, approval, and escalation. Not everyone needs to agree, but everyone must know who decides; threshold bands that define when decisions move up a level. Without thresholds, escalation becomes politics; and a decision log that captures date, decision, owner, rationale, and next review point. This turns governance into continuity.

The decision log is not paperwork. It is protection. It protects the organisation from rewriting history under pressure, and it protects leaders from making decisions in isolation without shared context.

The Board Interface: Trust Is a Design Outcome

Boards do not ask for more information because they love data. They ask for more information when they do not trust the information they are receiving, or when the narrative feels incomplete.

The CFO's legacy with the board is built through disciplined interface design: what the board must see, what leadership must own, and how the story is told consistently across cycles.

A mature board interface is structured around three layers of content:

Signals: the few metrics that indicate whether the enterprise is safe and on track, including liquidity, covenant headroom, cash conversion, margin bridge, and key risk indicators; drivers: what is causing the movement, focusing on the levers that explain reality such as volume, price, mix, productivity, churn, and working capital behaviour; and decisions: what leadership is doing about it, with clear actions, trade-offs, and implications for strategy and capital.

Boards do not want comfort. They want confidence. Confidence comes from coherence: stable definitions, repeated framing, disciplined explanation of variance, and visible governance around risk.

The CFO who builds a strong board interface leaves behind more than a pack format. They leave behind an expectation of truth-telling, and a shared language for performance that survives leadership transitions.

KPI Ownership and the End of Dashboard Theatre

Dashboards become theatre when they are filled with metrics that no one owns. Ownership is what turns a metric from wallpaper into action.

A legacy-grade KPI doctrine answers five questions for every critical metric:

Leaders typically ask the same questions: "Who owns the metric, and what decision rights come with that ownership?"; "What is the review cadence, and in which room does it become a decision?"; "What threshold triggers investigation, and what threshold triggers escalation?"; "What is the data lineage, and who is responsible for definition governance?"; and "What action is expected when the metric moves outside its band?"

When these questions are answered, the dashboard becomes an operating instrument. When they are not, the dashboard becomes a surface for debate.

The CFO's legacy is to make performance legible, actionable, and trusted. KPI ownership doctrine is one of the simplest ways to do it.

Capital Allocation as Covenant

Budgets and investment decisions are where leadership becomes visible. They are not only financial mechanisms. They are commitments the organisation can feel.

This is why the CFO's capital allocation philosophy is part of their legacy. It shapes what the enterprise becomes, and what it learns to protect.

In high-performing organisations, capital allocation follows a few consistent principles:

Protect the capability that produces differentiation: cost discipline should remove noise, not muscle. Fund what you claim: if leadership says innovation matters, it must be resourced with legitimacy, not symbolic residue. Make trade-offs explicit: when everything is a priority, nothing is. Design reinvestment rules: savings without reinvestment logic become short-term extraction, not transformation.

A CFO who codifies these principles creates stability in investment decisions across leadership cycles. The enterprise stops swinging between over-expansion and panic contraction. It becomes more mature in how it treats resources.

People Who Grow Because of You

As CFO, you manage numbers. But your real medium is people. Forecasts, dashboards, budgets, and models are produced by human judgement. If you want your work to endure, you must distribute capability, not concentrate it.

The CFOs who leave the strongest legacy are those who build a finance team that can think, not only execute. They develop successors deliberately. They teach non-finance leaders how to use financial information with confidence. They create an enterprise where financial intelligence is a shared capacity.

This is not a soft ambition. It is a strategic one. Capability is what protects the organisation when conditions change faster than process updates can keep up.

A practical development architecture includes:

A bench plan: named deputies for FP&A, controllership, business partnering, and systems governance, each with increasing decision exposure; a rotation path: finance talent moves through commercial, operations, and transformation work so they learn the business, not only the ledger; a narrative skill set: analysts learn to explain drivers and trade-offs to executives, not only to build slides; and a non-finance literacy programme: budget owners learn drivers, variances, and decision thresholds in their own language.

Every time you help a leader interpret their numbers without fear, you reduce the organisation's dependence on Finance. That is a legacy move. It turns Finance from gatekeeper into capability builder.

Capability Over Compliance

There is a difference between compliance and capability. Compliance is when departments submit budgets because they must. Capability is when leaders can articulate the drivers behind their numbers, explain variance without defensiveness, and make decisions using Finance as a partner rather than a policing function.

CFOs build capability. They do not settle for compliance.

Capability is built through repetition of good financial questions in the right rooms. Questions such as:

Leaders typically ask the same questions: "What is the driver, and what behaviour moves it?"; "What is the threshold, and what happens when we cross it?"; "What trade-off are we making, and what do we protect as non-negotiable?"; and "What is the next decision, and who owns it?"

When these questions become normal, financial maturity rises. Variance meetings shift from defence to action. Forecasting becomes a shared discipline. Escalation happens earlier. The CFO's influence increases not because of authority, but because the organisation becomes more intelligent with money.

The CFO as Culture Architect

Culture is not only a leadership function. It is a financial one. As CFO, you shape culture through what you approve, what you freeze, what you protect, and what you cut. You shape culture through the tone you set in reporting meetings: whether variance is treated as learning or blame.

You also shape culture through language. The language Finance uses in budgeting season becomes the emotional climate of accountability. If the language implies punishment, people hide. If the language implies stewardship, people engage.

A legacy-grade CFO protects two cultural assets relentlessly: truth and dignity.

Truth means financial integrity, clear definitions, and honest narratives. Dignity means discipline delivered with respect: decisions explained, trade-offs acknowledged, and people treated as partners rather than line items.

When truth and dignity are protected, the organisation becomes braver. It escalates earlier. It admits risk sooner. It adapts faster. That is not abstract culture. It is operational resilience.

Operationalising Legacy: The Legacy Playbook

Legacy becomes real only when it is operationalised. It cannot remain philosophical. The CFO who wants enduring impact must deliberately codify the work, institutionalise learning, and embed integrity infrastructure (Senge, 1990).

A practical Legacy Playbook includes six components.

In practice, this often looks like codify the rhythm: publish the annual cadence, the forecasting cycle, the performance review agenda, and escalation thresholds. Make them visible and stable; codify the language: define key terms in plain English. Forecast, budget, variance, risk, runway, and productivity should have stable meaning; codify the decision map: record who decides what, at what threshold, with what inputs, and where decisions are documented; codify the models: store driver assumptions, scenario logic, and bridge methodologies with clear ownership and update rules; institutionalise learning: run retrospectives after major cycles and disruptions, capture lessons, and update the playbook. Do not allow the enterprise to forget its scars; and embed integrity: align incentives with long-term thinking, protect whistleblowing and escalation pathways, and enforce definition governance so truth does not become negotiable.

This playbook is not bureaucracy. It is continuity. It ensures the organisation does not lose hard-won capability when people move on. It makes excellence repeatable.

Leaving Well: The Handover Is Part of the Work

Many leaders treat exit as a personal event. It is an organisational risk event. The quality of your handover determines whether your work becomes durable or collapses into improvisation.

A legacy-grade handover is not a folder of files. It is a structured transfer of context. It answers the questions your successor will need to lead, not just to administer.

A strong handover package typically includes:

The enterprise narrative: how the business makes money, what the current regime is, and where the real sensitivities sit; the truth dashboard: the five to ten metrics that define safety and performance, with definitions and threshold bands; the decision log: key decisions made in the last 12 to 24 months and their rationale, including what is due for review; the risk map: liquidity profile, covenant headroom, major exposures, and the early warning signals you trust; and the people map: who holds knowledge, who stabilises teams, where succession risk sits, and how to lead key relationships.

This is not self-importance. It is stewardship. When you leave well, you protect the organisation from unnecessary volatility, and you protect the integrity of what you built.

The Architecture Principles of Enduring CFO Work

If you strip away every tool and every project plan, legacy CFO work can be described as a set of design principles. These principles guide decisions when the organisation is tired, when politics rise, and when time is short. They also provide continuity when leadership changes.

Five principles appear repeatedly in organisations where finance remains coherent through transition.

In practice, this often looks like clarity: remove ambiguity. If a decision relies on interpretation, write the interpretation down and govern it; accountability with agency: assign ownership only where levers exist, and make shared costs transparent with explicit drivers; elasticity: design processes that can tighten and loosen without breaking. Cadence is a dial, not a switch; humanity: deliver discipline without humiliation. Fear makes numbers less accurate, not more accurate; and integrity: protect truth even when it is inconvenient. Without truth, the enterprise cannot lead itself.

These principles are not slogans. They are decision filters. When your successor faces a debate about whether to cut capability or protect it, these principles anchor the answer. When a leader wants to redefine a metric to improve optics, integrity blocks the move. When the organisation is exhausted, humanity keeps escalation alive.

Executive Case Insight: The CFO Who Built a System, Not a Shadow

Consider a mid-sized enterprise that had completed a successful turnaround. The CFO was widely respected and deeply involved. Forecasts were strong, liquidity was protected, and the board trusted the numbers.

When that CFO left, the organisation expected continuity. Instead, within two quarters, the forecast became inconsistent, cost conversations turned political, and the board began asking for increasingly detailed data.

The underlying issue was simple: the system had never been fully transferred. The rhythms lived in the CFO's calendar. The definitions lived in the CFO's head. The escalation paths relied on the CFO's personal relationships.

A new CFO arrived with strong technical competence, but they inherited dependence, not durability. They had to rebuild trust and re-codify what should have already been institutional.

The lesson is direct. If your work cannot survive your absence, it is not complete. The final phase of a transformation is not implementation. It is institutionalisation.

Institutionalisation looks like documented cadence, governed definitions, deputised ownership, and decision capture. It looks like a finance team that can explain drivers confidently without waiting for the CFO to interpret. It looks like a board interface that remains coherent even when the storyteller changes.

The Finance Function You Leave Behind

Legacy is also shaped by the operating model of Finance itself. A finance function can be efficient and still be fragile if capability is concentrated in a few individuals or if roles are built around heroic intervention.

A resilient finance operating model usually clarifies four domains:

Controllership: trusted close, disciplined controls, clean reconciliation, and audit readiness; FP&A and performance: driver-based planning, forecasting, scenario work, and decision framing; business partnering: embedded finance leaders who translate, challenge, and co-own outcomes with operational teams; and systems and data governance: ownership of definitions, KPI governance, data lineage, and dashboard integrity.

When these domains are clear, Finance becomes a system, not a set of personalities. When they are blurred, the organisation experiences Finance as inconsistent. Inconsistency is expensive. It creates rework, debate, and a slow erosion of credibility.

The CFO's role is to design this operating model so that it remains stable even as individuals move. That includes clear role charters, clean hand-offs between domains, and a culture where knowledge is shared rather than hoarded.

Institutional Integrity: When Incentives and Truth Collide

Finance integrity is not defended by good intentions. It is defended by infrastructure. The moment incentives and truth collide; the organisation will follow whichever is stronger.

This is why legacy CFOs build ethical infrastructure into ordinary routines. They ensure that performance incentives do not quietly reward value destruction. They ensure that risk is not punished for being visible. They ensure that controls are not bypassed for speed.

Ethical infrastructure includes incentive design that balances short-term output with long-term health. It includes governance that requires assumptions to be recorded and reviewed. It includes escalation pathways that protect those who raise concerns early. It includes a culture where numbers are corrected, not negotiated.

When ethical infrastructure exists, the organisation can move quickly without losing integrity. When it does not, speed becomes a liability. The enterprise starts optimising for optics and hiding its own weaknesses. That is how failures mature silently.

Your legacy is inseparable from the truth system you defended. Without truth, the enterprise cannot see itself. Without self-sight, it cannot lead.

The Legacy Scorecard: Twelve Questions to Test What You Leave Behind

If you want a simple way to assess whether your work is becoming durable, use a legacy scorecard. Ask these questions as if you were the next CFO inheriting the function.

Leaders typically ask the same questions: "Can I explain, in five minutes, how the business makes money, what the current operating regime is, and where the sensitivities sit?"; "Do the top metrics have stable definitions, owners, thresholds, and review cadence, or are they debated each month?"; "If volatility rises tomorrow, is there a documented shift to crisis cadence with clear triggers and escalation paths?"; "Can budget owners interpret their numbers without waiting for Finance to translate them?"; "Is there a decision log that records major trade-offs and rationale, or do we rely on memory and rumours?"; "Are shared service allocations transparent and governed, with visible drivers and a challenge process?"; "Can FP&A refresh scenarios quickly without rebuilding models from scratch?"; "Do controls and reconciliations protect integrity without creating bottlenecks that encourage workarounds?"; "Is the board pack coherent, consistent, and decision-oriented, or does it change shape with each presenter?"; "Is there a clear bench plan for critical finance roles, with genuine deputies and development exposure?"; "Are retrospectives and learning loops institutional, or do we move on and forget pain once it passes?"; and "When I leave, will the organisation have a playbook, or will it have a person-shaped hole?"

If you can answer these questions with confidence, you are building a legacy. If you cannot, you have identified your next build priorities. The scorecard is not for judgement; it is for stewardship.

A Letter to the Next CFO

If you want to crystallise your legacy work, write a letter to your successor. Not for publication. For continuity. The exercise forces clarity about what matters, what is fragile, and what must be protected.

A strong letter is not emotional. It is precise. It names the regime, the risks, the people, and the truths that are easy to miss in a handover pack.

It might begin like this: the organisation runs well when cadence is kept, definitions are governed, and variance is translated into decisions quickly. It becomes fragile when performance reviews turn into blame, when forecasts are treated as renegotiation, or when shared costs become political.

It might include this warning: protect integrity first. Do not allow the enterprise to trade truth for comfort. The day the numbers become negotiable is the day leadership becomes performative.

And it might include this invitation: build on what works, refine what does not, and never let the system become dependent on your personality. Your job is to make the organisation more capable, not more impressed.

This is the mindset of legacy CFO leadership. You are not guarding an empire. You are stewarding an operating system for the people who will carry it next.

The Exit Horizon: Institutionalisation Before Transition

Legacy does not begin when you resign. It begins the moment you realise that every system must be survivable. The most effective CFOs treat institutionalisation as a standing workstream, not a late-stage scramble.

A practical approach is to manage an "exit horizon" even when you have no intention of leaving. It is a 180-day rolling view of what would become fragile if you disappeared tomorrow. This horizon becomes a stewardship discipline: the work of removing single points of failure.

An exit horizon plan typically includes three themes.

In practice, this often looks like remove hero dependency: identify processes or relationships that only work because one person remembers the context, and convert that context into shared assets; strengthen deputies: ensure key finance leaders can run the cadence, present to executives, and handle escalation without the CFO acting as translator; and simplify and govern: reduce complexity where it does not create decision value, and govern what must remain complex through clear ownership and rules.

The exit horizon is not a disengagement mechanism. It is an excellence mechanism. Organisations that institutionalise early move faster, because they are not rebuilding trust every time a person changes role.

What to Preserve and What to Evolve

A frequent mistake in leadership transition is to treat legacy as preservation. The goal is not to freeze your way of working. The goal is to preserve the principles that keep the organisation coherent, while allowing methods to evolve.

There are usually three categories.

In practice, this often looks like preserve the principles: integrity, clear definitions, disciplined cadence, explicit trade-offs, and dignity in delivery; evolve the methods: tools, dashboards, workflow automation, reporting formats, and team structures will change as the business changes; and replace the personality: your successor will lead differently. The system must not require them to mimic you. It must require them to honour the principles.

If the organisation confuses method with principle, it will either resist improvement or destroy what was working. A legacy-grade CFO names the difference clearly so that the next era can progress without losing coherence.

The CFO's Legacy Commitments

Every CFO can choose the commitments that define their tenure. These commitments are not public statements. They are operational promises you keep repeatedly, even when pressure is high.

In organisations that remain healthy through change, CFO legacy commitments often include:

We will tell the truth early, even when it is uncomfortable. We will protect liquidity and integrity as non-negotiables. We will design governance so decisions are clear, not political. We will treat forecasting as reality, not as a negotiation. We will cut cost with dignity and explain trade-offs openly. We will build capability so the organisation becomes financially intelligent without fear.

These commitments are practical. They show up in meeting tone, in budgeting language, in escalation responses, in how reports are framed, and in who receives support under pressure. If you hold these commitments, you leave behind a culture that is harder to corrupt.

When Legacy Fails: Warning Signs to Watch

It is also useful to name the warning signs that indicate legacy is weakening. They rarely appear as headline failures. They appear as small shifts in behaviour that, over time, erode integrity and speed.

Watch for signs such as:

Numbers become a debate rather than a shared reference point; forecasts are adjusted late to reduce accountability rather than early to improve decision-making; managers stop escalating risk until the last possible moment; definitions drift quietly, and different teams report different versions of the same metric; and shadow reporting re-emerges because leaders do not trust the official view.

When these signs appear, it is tempting to blame people. The stronger move is to repair the system. Most of these behaviours are rational responses to unclear governance or fear. Legacy leadership means you repair the environment, so truth becomes safe again.

Legacy Summary

If you had to compress your legacy into a single page for your successor, it would not be a list of projects. It would be a summary of what must remain true for the enterprise to stay coherent.

That page might read as follows. Keep cadence predictable. Keep definitions governed. Keep decision rights explicit. Keep escalation safe. Keep the board interface consistent. Keep liquidity protected. Keep dignity intact when cost pressure rises. Keep learning loops alive so the organisation does not repeat avoidable pain.

If those truths remain, your successor can change tools, change reporting formats, restructure teams, and still preserve the enterprise's financial maturity. If those truths are lost, the organisation will revert to theatre and improvisation, regardless of what technology it buys.

Legacy, in the end, is not the elegance of your framework. It is the durability of your truth.

The Quiet Mark of Executive Maturity

At a certain level, success is no longer measured only by your performance. It is measured by what becomes possible in others because of how you built. That is the quiet mark of executive maturity.

You see it when an operational leader challenges their own assumptions using driver logic without being prompted. You see it when a business partner escalates risk early because the system makes it safe. You see it when the board discussion centres on choices and consequences, not on questioning the validity of the numbers.

You also see it when the organisation faces stress and, instead of fracturing, it tightens into clarity: the right rooms, the right cadence, the right thresholds, the same definitions, and a disciplined record of what is being decided.

That is what you are building throughout this book. Not a collection of finance techniques, but a durable executive operating system that turns uncertainty into structured action.

If you are ever unsure what to prioritise next, return to a single question: what would make this enterprise clearer, calmer, and more honest when you are not present? Build that. Every time you remove ambiguity, improve interpretability, or protect integrity, you extend the half-life of your leadership. That is what it means to build for endurance, not applause.

Final Thesis: The CFO's Real Output

The ultimate output of a CFO is not a report. It is not a budget. It is not even a transformation programme.

The ultimate output is an organisation that can see itself clearly, decide with maturity, and remain coherent under pressure.

When you build systems that are durable, you give the enterprise a spine. When you build people who are capable, you give the enterprise a nervous system. When you build integrity into governance and language, you give the enterprise a conscience.

That is the true executive thesis of financial orchestration: leadership that outlives the leader.

From Control to Composition

Financial orchestration begins with a simple shift in identity. The CFO is no longer only the person who protects the integrity of the numbers. The modern CFO designs the conditions in which the organisation can see clearly, decide coherently, and keep moving when reality changes.

Across this book, that design has taken practical form. Budgeting became an operating rhythm rather than a seasonal negotiation. Cost centres became an architecture of accountability rather than a coding exercise. FP&A platforms became decision infrastructure rather than software implementations. Change management became part of finance leadership rather than a communication task handed to someone else. Cost culture became visible as a force that shapes behaviour. Dashboards became instruments for attention and action. Governance became the structure that protects speed. Crisis revealed whether those structures were real. And legacy became the test of whether the system can continue without depending on the person who built it.

This is the movement from control to composition. Control asks whether rules were followed. Composition asks whether the parts of the enterprise are arranged so that good decisions can happen repeatedly. It does not abandon control; it puts control in service of a larger operating design.

The difference is visible in the rooms where work happens. A budget review no longer begins with defence of line items but with the drivers that moved and the choices now available. A forecast is not treated as a promise that must be protected from reality, but as an updated view used to direct attention. A dashboard does not win because it contains more metrics; it wins because it makes the next decision easier to see. A governance mechanism does not prove its value by creating more approvals; it proves its value by making authority, escalation, and boundaries unmistakable.

The same principle applies under pressure. When volatility rises, organisations often respond by inventing new meetings, new reports, and new controls. That can create the appearance of action while destroying decision capacity. A well-orchestrated finance system does something different. It tightens the existing rhythm. It shortens the distance between signal and decision. It makes the critical boundaries more visible. It preserves one set of definitions. It records what has been decided and why. It keeps the enterprise from fragmenting into private versions of reality.

Technology raises the standard further. AI, copilots, forecasting models, and automated commentary can compress analytical work dramatically. They can also produce confidence faster than they produce truth. The finance function therefore needs the same disciplines around model-produced outputs that it applies to material financial information: traceability, ownership, review, escalation, and explicit limits on where judgement may be delegated. The goal is not to resist automation. It is to ensure that automation strengthens the operating system rather than creating a shadow one.

At the highest level, the CFO becomes a composer of organisational clarity. You design cadence: when information arrives, when assumptions are refreshed, and when decisions return to the room. You design language: which definitions are authoritative and how changes are governed. You design visibility: what leaders must see early and what can remain detail. You design accountability: who owns the outcome, who owns the data, and where authority changes under stress. You design memory: decision logs, model registers, reconciliations, and handover artefacts that stop the organisation from relearning the same lessons through pain.

That work is often quiet. There may be no dramatic moment when the enterprise announces that its decision architecture has improved. Instead, meetings become shorter. Variances are explained earlier. Leaders stop arguing about whose number is correct. Teams understand what they own. Escalation carries less emotional charge because the thresholds were agreed before the pressure arrived. The board receives fewer surprises. Finance spends less time reconstructing the past and more time helping the business choose what happens next.

This is also the human side of orchestration. Ambiguity is expensive. It consumes attention, creates defensive behaviour, and makes capable people hesitate. Clear systems reduce that tax. They do not remove uncertainty, but they make uncertainty governable. People know where to look, what language to use, who decides, and what happens when the assumptions change.

The final test is whether the architecture survives you. If the budgeting rhythm collapses when a particular leader leaves, it was a habit, not a system. If the KPI definitions live in one analyst's memory, they are not governed. If the board narrative depends on the CFO personally translating every number, capability has not yet been embedded. Legacy-grade finance converts personal excellence into institutional capacity.

So the measure of the modern CFO is not how indispensable the CFO becomes. It is how much clarity, judgement, and disciplined movement the organisation can sustain without constant rescue. Build the system so that others can use it. Teach the language until it becomes shared. Protect the definitions until they become trusted. Create the rhythms until they become normal. Develop people until they can challenge the model rather than merely receive it.

That is the true output of financial orchestration: an enterprise that can see itself clearly, make difficult choices without losing coherence, and remain governable when conditions are no longer comfortable. The numbers still matter. Control still matters. Precision still matters. But their highest value is realised when they become part of an operating architecture that helps people decide and act well.

Build that architecture carefully. Then let it work.

Appendix A – Budget Orchestration Toolkit

These templates convert budgeting into an executable rhythm: clear decision moments, consistent submissions, and a forecast cadence that protects both commitment and agility.

A1. Annual Budget Calendar Template

Use this calendar to design around decision moments (when leadership must choose), not submission moments (when spreadsheets are collected). Populate timing to match operational seasonality.

Table A.1 – Set Direction (Alignment + Assumptions + Guidance)

Phase / Stage	Decision moment	Owner(s)	Primary output	Timing (month/week)	Dependencies / notes
Strategic pre-alignment	Confirm enterprise priorities and constraints	CEO/CFO/ Exec team	Budget thesis + guardrails		
Assumption spine	Lock key assumptions and external scenario set	CFO/FP&A	Assumption pack + scenario ranges		
Guidance release	Issue guidance with narrative and targets	CFO	Budget narrative pack		

Table A.2 – Build the Plan (Department Planning + Calibration)

Phase / Stage	Decision moment	Owner(s)	Primary output	Timing (month/week)	Dependencies / notes
Department planning	Departments build plans against drivers	Budget owners	Department submission (drivers + initiatives)		
Calibration round 1	Resolve cross-functional dependencies	CFO/Finance partners	Trade-offs list + revised submissions		
Calibration round 2	Finalise targets, CapEx, headcount	Exec team	Final budget proposal		

Table A.3 – Govern + Run It (Approval + Embed + Refresh + Learning)

Phase / Stage	Decision moment	Owner(s)	Primary output	Timing (month/week)	Dependencies / notes
Approval forum	Formal approval and accountability reset	Board/CEO/CFO	Approved budget + governance cadence		
Launch & embed	Translate budget into operating rhythm	CFO/COO/HR	Targets cascaded + meeting rhythm		
Quarterly refresh	Refresh forecast and revalidate assumptions	FP&A/Exec team	Rolling forecast + trigger actions		
Year-end learning	Capture decisions and improvement actions	CFO/FP&A	Budget lessons log + next-year upgrades		

A2. Department Submission Structure

Use this structure to prevent 'spreadsheet-only' budgets. The submission is a narrative plus drivers, with clear trade-offs and dependencies.

Submission component	What it must contain	Owner	Quality test
Operating thesis	What the department is trying to achieve this year, and what it will stop doing	Department head	Reads like a plan, not a defence
Driver model	Volume/price/mix assumptions, productivity drivers, service levels	Budget owner + FP&A	Drivers link to numbers and can be stress-tested
Resource plan	Headcount, contractors, key hires, capability gaps	Department head + HR	Roles are tied to outcomes, not titles
Initiatives & ROI	Top initiatives, cost-to-deliver, expected benefit, timing	Department leads	Benefits and timing are explicit, not implied
Risks & contingencies	Top risks, triggers, and first actions if conditions tighten	Department head	Risk is escalated early and documented
Cross-functional dependencies	What this plan requires from other teams	Department head	Dependencies are surfaced before approval

Narrative prompt:

Prompt	Department response
Intent in one sentence	
The three drivers that matter most	
The two biggest risks and earliest triggers	
What we will protect if conditions tighten	
What we will stop, pause, or defer first	
Where we need decisions or support	

A3. Forecast Review Cadence

Use this cadence to keep forecasting real: the same assumptions, the same decision forums, and clear trigger points for escalation.

Cadence	Forum / purpose	Participants	Inputs	Outputs	Escalation rule
Weekly (leading indicators)	Scan signals and risks early	Ops leads + FP&A	KPIs, sales pipeline, operational constraints	Early warnings + next actions	Escalate if thresholds breached
Monthly (performance rhythm)	Translate results into decisions	Exec team + FP&A	Close results, variance drivers, cash bridge	Decision log updates + actions	Escalate decisions above threshold bands
Quarterly (directional rhythm)	Refresh forecast and scenarios	Exec team + FP&A	Updated assumptions, scenario ranges	Rolling forecast + trigger actions	Switch cadence in volatility regimes
Ad hoc (triggered)	Respond to defined triggers	Decision owners	Trigger sheet, options, trade-offs	Decision + communication	Use escalation map and timeboxes
Board cadence	Board visibility and accountability	Board/CEO/CFO	Signals, drivers, decisions	Board pack + approvals	Document rationale and next review date

Appendix B – Cost Centre Transformation Pack

These templates support cost centre redesign as a governance exercise: clear ownership, clean mapping, and auditable allocation logic.

B1. Old-to-New Mapping Template

Use this to preserve comparability during transition. Record the mapping rule, effective date, and restatement approach to prevent 'two truths' during reporting.

Old code / name	New code / name	Mapping rule	Owner	Effective date	Restatement approach	Notes

B2. Cost Centre Ownership Sheet

Use this sheet to make accountability real. The owner must have influence over the cost levers, and Finance must know the escalation route for exceptions.

Field	**Entry**
Cost centre	
Owner	
Scope (included / excluded)	
Controllable levers	
Review cadence	
Escalation thresholds	
Finance partner	
Notes	

B3. Reallocation Audit Checklist

Use this checklist before any reallocation or allocation-logic change to preserve trust, auditability, and decision clarity.

Check	Evidence / notes
Driver logic is documented (why this allocation exists)	
Owners of sending and receiving cost centres have been informed	
Approval route followed (per governance thresholds)	
Effective period and reversibility are defined	
Comparability impact assessed (variance narrative updated)	
Systems and master data updated consistently	
Dashboards and KPI definitions updated if impacted	
Decision recorded in decision log (rationale + next review)	
Post-entry reconciliation completed (no orphan costs)	
Communication issued to affected leaders (what changed, what to watch)	

B4. Cost Centre Diagnostic and Governance Checklists

Use these as blank-form prompts during redesign. Record evidence, decisions, and required actions. For the underlying cost-centre doctrine, see Chapter 3.

Diagnostic prompts

□ Which decisions must the cost-centre structure support?
□ Where does accountability sit without matching influence?
□ Which shared costs require a governed allocation rule?
□ Which legacy codes can be retired?
□ Which mappings require historical restatement or bridge reporting?

Governance prompts

□ Named owner for every active cost centre.
□ Documented allocation method and review date.
□ Change authority and effective-date rule.
□ Exception and escalation route.
□ Post-implementation review after the first full reporting cycle.

Appendix C – FP&A System Transition Playbook

These tools support a controlled transition: phased delivery, accountable champions, and migration discipline that prevents 'go-live theatre'.

C1. Phased Implementation Roadmap

Use this roadmap to separate technical delivery from operational adoption. Each phase should have explicit success criteria and a decision to proceed.

Table C.1 – Foundation + Pilot

Phase	Objective	Key activities	Deliverables	Success criteria	Key risks / mitigations
Foundation	Stabilise data, definitions, and governance	Data inventory; master data owners; KPI definitions; environment setup	Data model + governance baseline	Single source definitions agreed; owners named	Definition drift / lock change control
Pilot	Prove the model with one unit	Configure pilot; migrate sample; UAT; train pilot users	Pilot dashboards + forecast process	Pilot runs the rhythm without shadow reporting	Pilot too 'special' / enforce standard artefacts

Table C.2 – Expand + Integrate + Embed

Phase	Objective	Key activities	Deliverables	Success criteria	Key risks / mitigations
Expand	Scale to core functions	Iterate; onboard functions; integrate drivers	Scaled forecasting + reporting	Usage in leadership forums; consistent assumptions	Change fatigue / cadence discipline
Integrate	Link to upstream/downstream systems	Interfaces; automation; security; audit trails	Integrated data pipelines	Reduced manual work; clear lineage	Data quality / implement monitoring
Embed	Make it the standard operating rhythm	Transition ownership; retire old tools; enforce governance	Go-live + decommission plan	No parallel truth; adoption non-negotiables met	Shadow reporting / enforce escalation route

C2. Champion Model

Use the champion model to distribute capability. Champions own local adoption and feedback, while the central team owns standards and decision rights.

Role	Primary responsibilities	Time commitment	Success measures
Executive sponsor	Protect priority; remove blockers; enforce non-negotiables		Adoption sustained; escalation used early
Finance product owner	Own process design; backlog; release decisions		Stable cadence; minimal rework
Data / IT owner	Own integrations, security, and lineage		Data quality monitored; issues resolved quickly
Functional champions	Translate process into daily work; coach users		Local adoption; reduced helpdesk dependency
Super users	Hands-on support; training; early warning feedback		Fast issue resolution; confidence rises
Change lead	Communication rhythm; training plan; adoption tracking		Clear narrative; resistance addressed early
PMO / delivery lead	Plan, milestones, risk register, governance forums		Phases delivered; decisions timeboxed

C3. Data Migration Checklist

Use this checklist to prevent data chaos and post-go-live distrust. Migration is not a technical task; it is a credibility task.

Step	Evidence / notes
Inventory all source data sets and owners	
Map fields and definitions to the target model	
Clean and standardise master data (cost centres, products, entities)	
Define reconciliation rules and tolerance thresholds	
Run test migration and reconcile results	
Document exceptions and remediation actions	
Complete user acceptance testing against real decisions	
Lock change control for definitions and mappings	
Execute cutover plan with rollback criteria	
Confirm audit trail and lineage documentation	
Decommission or freeze old reporting tools per plan	

C4. Change and Adoption Prompts

Use these prompts as a working adoption sheet. For the underlying change-leadership guidance, see Chapter 5.

Readiness check

□ Executive sponsor visible and active.
□ Local champions named.
□ Training mapped by role.
□ Support clinics scheduled.
□ Legacy process retirement date agreed.

Adoption rhythm

□ Pre-launch: orient and test.
□ Weeks 1–2: protect trust and resolve blockers.
□ Weeks 3–4: stabilise behaviours.
□ Weeks 5–8: tighten routines and ownership.
□ Weeks 9–12: codify, measure, and normalise.

Communication check

□ What is changing?
□ Why now?
□ What must each role do differently?
□ Where can people get help?
□ What will stop after go-live?

Quick adoption checks

Readiness check	Adoption rhythm	Communication check
• □ Executive sponsor visible and active. • □ Local champions named. • □ Training mapped by role. • □ Support clinics scheduled. • □ Legacy process retirement date agreed.	• □ Pre-launch: orient and test. • □ Weeks 1–2: protect trust and resolve blockers. • □ Weeks 3–4: stabilise behaviours. • □ Weeks 5–8: tighten routines and ownership. • □ Weeks 9–12: codify, measure, and normalise.	• □ What is changing? • □ Why now? • □ What must each role do differently? • □ Where can people get help? • □ What will stop after go-live?

1. Readiness, narrative, and standards

Area	Prompts / indicators	Notes
Confusion indicators	• People do not know which numbers to trust. • People do not know what "good" looks like in the new process. • People do not know whether mistakes will be punished or treated as learning. • People do not know which process is temporary and which is now the standard. • People do not know who to ask, so they stop asking.	
Change readiness scan	• Change load: how many other programmes are currently running, and whether the organisation is already fatigued. • Trust level: whether people believe leadership tells the truth when pressure rises. • Capability baseline: whether managers can interpret financial information without relying on Finance to translate every line. • Data hygiene: whether the underlying inputs are stable enough to support a single view without constant manual correction. • Consequence clarity: whether people know how performance will be assessed during the transition.	
Change narrative	• What is changing? • Why does it matter now? • What does success look like in daily work? • What happens next, and how will we be supported?	
Confidence questions	• What do I do differently now? • How do I know I am doing it correctly? • What happens if I make a mistake? • Who helps me when I get stuck? • What is the fastest way to get this done without reverting to the old method?	
CFO non-negotiables	• One shared forecast. One set of assumptions. No private alternative numbers used for executive decisions. • One decision surface. Dashboards and reporting views used in leadership forums must be the same ones used by budget owners. • One route for exceptions. If a team cannot comply, they escalate early, and the exception is documented with a path back to standard. • One vocabulary. If Finance uses one term and Operations uses another, you will spend your time resolving language, not performance.	

2. Coalition and adoption rhythms

Area	Prompts / indicators	Notes
Coalition of influencers	• Budget owners and high-influence managers. • Practical operators who know how work actually gets done. • Analysts and super-users who will become informal teachers. • HR and People partners who can see the human temperature. • Procurement and IT leaders who control connected workflows.	
Executive rhythm	• A fortnightly Steering Group, chaired by the CFO, focused on decisions and escalations. • A monthly executive review that uses the new dashboards as the default decision surface. • A board update rhythm that focuses on risk, liquidity, delivery milestones, and adoption integrity.	
Manager rhythm	• Weekly team-level check-ins: what is working, what is unclear, what support is needed. • A consistent monthly variance and forecast rhythm, using the new logic and definitions. • A short escalation route for blockers that managers cannot resolve alone.	
User rhythm	• Weekly office hours in the first twelve weeks. • A champions sync that captures friction points and improvement requests. • Micro-learning refreshes at week four, week eight, and week twelve, based on what users are actually struggling with.	

3. The 90-day adoption arc

Area	Prompts / indicators	Notes
Days 1–30: Orientation	• Keep office hours weekly and respond quickly to common friction. • Publish short clarifications fast, and update guides when the reality changes. • Run executive reviews using the new dashboards, even if imperfect, so the organisation sees commitment. • Maintain reconciliation views where necessary, but time-box them.	
Days 31–60: Stabilisation	• Reduce friction points surfaced in the first month. • Tighten definitions and remove duplicate templates. • Move from "how to use" questions to "how to interpret" coaching. • Begin tracking adoption metrics and addressing gaps through support, not shame.	
Days 61–90: Optimisation	• Codify the most effective practices into the permanent operating cadence. • Decommission legacy reports and shadow templates. • Strengthen governance triggers and escalation pathways. • Introduce capability upgrades, such as driver-based forecasting refinements, scenario refresh routines, and sharper dashboards.	

4. Change cadence by phase

Area	Prompts / indicators	Notes
Pre-launch: 4–6 weeks before go-live	• Announce the narrative and the timeline. • Identify champions and run preview sessions. • Publish the "what changes for you" guide by role. • Run a live demo for leadership and budget owners, using real examples. • Open the help route and confirm response times.	
Weeks 1–2: Go-live and initial adoption	• Daily or every-other-day leadership check-ins for the core decision group, focused on blockers and integrity risks. • Two office-hour slots per week, then reduce as confidence rises. • A short end-of-week update: what changed, what stabilised, what we fixed, what happens next.	
Weeks 3–4: Stabilise behaviours	• Move office hours to weekly. • Begin simple adoption reporting: participation, submission timeliness, major friction categories. • Run the first retrospective with champions and managers, then publish the improvements.	
Weeks 5–8: Tighten and embed	• Shift from support-heavy to coaching-heavy. • Lock definitions and reduce reconciliation views. • Begin decommissioning legacy templates in phases. • Hold a leadership calibration session: what is the new decision rhythm, and what is now the standard.	
Weeks 9–12: Codify and normalise	• Convert lessons into permanent guidance. • Formalise the ongoing cadence for forecast refresh and variance action. • Close out the change programme with an explicit "now standard" communication: what is final, what is evolving, and how improvements will be governed.	

5. Communication and manager cascade

Area	Prompts / indicators	Notes
Weekly progress update	• What changed since last week? • What is stable? • What happens next? • What support is available? • What did we learn and adjust?	
Outcome language	• "Forecast refresh is now two days, not seven." • "Budget owners can see spend drivers without waiting for Finance." • "We reduced manual reclassifications by half." • "Variance conversations are shifting from explanation to action."	
Manager cascade Q&A	• What changes for our team this month? • What does good look like while we learn? • What happens if we get it wrong? • Where do we get help? • What is not changing?	

Appendix D – Governance & Dashboard Templates

These templates govern definitions, decision rights, escalation, and dashboard architecture. Used consistently, they prevent drift, shadow reporting, and political decision-making.

D1. RACI Structure Template

Populate this RACI for the decisions and artefacts that create ambiguity. Keep it short: govern what is expensive when unclear.

Table D.1 – Planning + Financial Control Decisions

Process / decision	R	A	C	I	Cadence	Escalation threshold / route
Budget guidance & targets						
Forecast revisions & scenarios						
Cost centre change control						
Allocation logic changes						
Investment approvals (CapEx)						

Table D.2 – Performance + Data + Operating Governance

Process / decision	R	A	C	I	Cadence	Escalation threshold / route
KPI definition changes						
Dashboard architecture & change control						
Headcount approvals						
Master data governance						

D2. KPI Governance Sheet

Use one sheet per KPI. The goal is coherence: the same metric means the same thing in every room, with a known owner and change control.

KPI	Purpose / decision it supports	Owner	Definition (included / excluded)	Data source(s)	Refresh cadence	Thresholds / targets	Change control owner

D3. Decision Escalation Map

Use this map to make escalation safe and fast. Thresholds prevent politics; timeboxes prevent drift; the decision log creates continuity.

Decision type	**Tier**	**Threshold trigger**	**Decision owner**	**Required inputs**	**Timebox**	**Documentation**
Operational adjustment	1					Decision log entry
Budget reallocation / trade-off	2					Decision log + impact note
Material forecast revision	3					Decision log + scenario rationale
Strategic or capital decision	4					Decision memo + board visibility

D4. Dashboard Architecture Template

Design dashboards as decision engines. Build layers by audience and keep the 'signals–drivers–decisions' structure consistent.

Layer / audience	**Primary decisions supported**	**Key questions**	**Core KPIs (signals)**	**Driver views**	**Update cadence**	**Owner**
Board						
Executive leadership						
Functional leaders						
Operational teams						

D5. Reference Checklists and Doctrines

Use this page as a governance health check. For the underlying governance, crisis, and legacy principles, see Chapters 8–10.

Governance health check

□ Decision rights are explicit for high-cost ambiguity.
□ Escalation thresholds are visible and time-bound.
□ Board and audit committee packs use governed definitions.
□ Critical KPIs have business owners and data owners.
□ Capital decisions reference agreed gates and assumptions.
□ Finance capability is documented beyond individual people.

Legacy test

□ The rhythm continues without the current CFO.
□ Definitions survive personnel changes.
□ Decision history can be reconstructed.
□ Critical models and reports have named owners.
□ Successors can locate the operating doctrine.
□ The function can tighten under stress without inventing a new system.

Glossary

Accountability: Clear responsibility for an outcome, matched with sufficient authority, information, and escalation rights.

Anchor metric: A small number of outcome measures that orient executive attention.

Assumption spine: The governed set of planning assumptions shared across budgeting, forecasting, and scenarios.

Cadence: The recurring rhythm through which information is refreshed, reviewed, challenged, and converted into decisions.

Calibration: The process of reconciling top-down ambition with bottom-up operating reality.

Contingency reserve: Deliberately held capacity or funding released only through defined governance.

Cost culture: The shared beliefs and behaviours that shape how an organisation interprets and manages cost.

Cost centre: A financial responsibility unit used to make cost ownership and reporting legible.

Decision engine: A system that converts signals into interpretation, choice, action, and learning.

Decision log: A record of what was decided, why, which assumptions supported it, and what would cause revisit.

Decision rights: The explicit authority to make, approve, challenge, or escalate a decision.

Doctrine: A repeatable governing rule that protects decision quality across changing circumstances.

Driver: An operational variable that causally influences a financial or performance outcome.

Driver tree: A map connecting financial outcomes to the operational variables that create them.

Escalation threshold: A visible condition that moves a decision to a higher level of authority.

Forecast: The current view of what is likely to happen if known conditions and actions persist.

Governance: The architecture of authority, information, review, challenge, escalation, and accountability.

Guardrail: A rule or boundary that enables delegated action without losing enterprise coherence.

Integrity: The condition in which definitions, sources, transformations, controls, and accountability support trust in the output.

KPI governance: The ownership, definition, lineage, refresh, change control, and action logic attached to a critical metric.

Lever: A variable leadership can actively change to influence an outcome.

Lineage: The traceable path from authoritative source data through transformation to a reported or model-produced output.

Materiality: The level at which a variance, risk, or decision becomes significant enough to require a different review or authority.

Model register: A governed record of material analytical or AI models, their purpose, owner, version, validation, limitations, and review requirements.

Operating posture: The practical stance leadership adopts in response to prevailing conditions, risk, and available capacity.

Orchestration: The deliberate coordination of financial structures, rhythms, systems, people, and governance so decisions remain coherent.

Planning stack: The layers that turn source-system data into governed models, dashboards, narratives, and decisions.

Reconciliation: The process of proving that outputs agree to authoritative sources or explaining and governing legitimate differences.

Regime: A distinct operating condition that changes decision rules, cadence, or resource posture.

Scenario: A coherent alternative set of assumptions applied to the same underlying model or driver structure.

Semantic layer: The governed definitions and calculation logic that give shared meaning to data across tools and reports.

Shared fact base: The governed set of facts and definitions used as the common starting point for executive decisions.

Signal: A change in data, behaviour, or conditions that may require interpretation or action.

Stewardship: Leadership responsibility for protecting resources, integrity, capability, and long-term institutional health.

Trigger: A visible, measurable condition that causes a pre-agreed review, action, or escalation.

Variance: The difference between expected and actual performance, interpreted through drivers rather than treated as explanation by itself.

Further Reading and Reference Frameworks

These works and frameworks provide supporting context for the governance, decision, change, measurement, and AI-risk principles used throughout this volume.

COSO (2013). Internal Control—Integrated Framework. Committee of Sponsoring Organizations of the Treadway Commission.

Davenport, T. H. and Harris, J. G. (2007). Competing on Analytics. Harvard Business School Press.

Edmondson, A. C. (1999). Psychological Safety and Learning Behavior in Work Teams. Administrative Science Quarterly, 44(2), 350–383.

Edmondson, A. C. (2019). The Fearless Organization. Wiley.

Hope, J. and Fraser, R. (2003). Beyond Budgeting. Harvard Business School Press.

ISO/IEC 42001:2023. Information technology — Artificial intelligence — Management system.

Kahneman, D. (2011). Thinking, Fast and Slow. Farrar, Straus and Giroux.

Kaplan, R. S. and Norton, D. P. (1996). The Balanced Scorecard. Harvard Business School Press.

Kotter, J. P. (1996). Leading Change. Harvard Business School Press.

NIST (2023). Artificial Intelligence Risk Management Framework (AI RMF 1.0), NIST AI 100-1.

NIST (2024). Artificial Intelligence Risk Management Framework: Generative Artificial Intelligence Profile, NIST AI 600-1.

OECD (2019). Recommendation of the Council on Artificial Intelligence. OECD Legal Instruments.

Senge, P. M. (1990). The Fifth Discipline. Doubleday.

Weick, K. E. and Sutcliffe, K. M. (2007). Managing the Unexpected, 2nd ed. Jossey-Bass.

World Economic Forum (2020). The Future of Jobs Report 2020. World Economic Forum.

With Gratitude

To every finance leader quietly holding up the architecture of a company,
this book was written for you.

To the teams who challenged, trusted, and partnered with me through system changes, budget cycles, late nights, and strategic pivots, thank you for showing me what real orchestration looks like.

To the voices that encouraged me to write not just from the head, but from the heart,
you helped shape every chapter.

To my spirit familia and unseen mentors,
your guidance turned process into purpose, and clarity into courage.

And finally, to those who believe that spreadsheets can serve people, that dashboards can spark decisions, and that Finance can be a form of leadership,
this is your legacy, too.

About the Author

Dr. Leticia Lilleström is a strategic finance leader, published author, and organisational change architect with a PhD in Executive Leadership and over a decade of experience driving financial transformation across sectors.

With a background spanning corporate finance, cross-functional budgeting, and systems leadership, Leticia brings a rare blend of analytical rigour, human insight, and visionary clarity to the evolving CFO role.

She is the creator of *The Strategic CFO* series, a trilogy exploring the transformation of modern finance from control to capability, from silence to stewardship.

Leticia also hosts the podcast *The Heart Advantage*, where financial and executive leadership meet emotional intelligence, intuition, and the future of decision-making.

Through her books, advisory work, and speaking engagements, Leticia continues to redefine what it means to lead not just by numbers, but by narrative, nuance, and next-level thinking.

www.ingramcontent.com/pod-product-compliance
Lightning Source LLC
Chambersburg PA
CBHW041301210926
51847CB00010B/102